HAUNTED INDIANA 3

Mark Marimen

Introduction by
Chris Woodyard

Haunted Indiana 3 ©2001 by Mark Marimen

Printed in the United States of America

05 04 03   5 4 3 2

ISBN 1-882376-81-1

Cover photograph through the kind courtesy of the
      Walter A. Reeder, Jr., Family
Cover design by Adventures with Nature, East Lansing, Michigan

Holt, Michigan

Other titles in the Thunder Bay Press *Tales of the Supernatural* series:
   Haunted Indiana (by Mark Marimen)
   Haunted Indiana 2 (by Mark Marimen)
   School Spirits (by Mark Marimen)
   Chicagoland Ghosts
   Haunts of the Upper Great Lakes
   Michigan Haunts and Hauntings

CONTENTS

DEDICATION

In my limited experience, dedicating a book is one of the most daunting tasks that comes with writing. There are simply so many people who deserve to have whatever dubious "honor" comes with such a dedication.

Never the less, this book is lovingly dedicated to my wife Jane, who fills my life with more joy than I can ever deserve and to Abby, who makes that life complete. I love you both more than I can ever say.

This book is also dedicated to Bill and Patty Wilkins, who gave me that life and to whom I owe all that I am. You really are the best.

Finally, this book is dedicated to a close circle of friends, especially Jeremy and Julia, who are daily my cohorts in crime, and who fill my life with laughter and light. Thanks—I am thankful to God for having been blessed with you.

—*Mark Marimen*

INTRODUCTION

Why do we like to be frightened by ghost stories? I think it is a part of what makes us human. Ghost stories help us confront and conquer our fears. They scare us safely—like riding the roller coaster at the amusement park. They also connect us with the world of our ancestors, the world of the dead.

And it is connection that Mark Marimen recognizes. Here you'll find history—and mystery. Here you'll find not only the old folktales told around the campfire, but the stories of people who have experienced ghostly horrors for themselves. Here you'll find the ancient legends brought to all-too-real life in the twenty-first century.

We humans need to be scared. Life for primitive man was full of terror—the gnawing cold, hunger clawing at the belly, those glowing eyes just outside the ring of light cast by the fire. Man was conditioned to come alive at the first scent of danger, to be on the edge—all senses scanning the dark. But we have been tamed. And the price we pay for full bellies and central heating is a world of danger outside our control. A world where we may simply curl up and sleep, as domesticated as dogs.

Perhaps we need those eyes beyond the circle of firelight to feel truly human. Let us sit down by the fire and listen to the old tales, the new tales—and the *scary* tales in that state of terror, Haunted Indiana.

—Chris Woodyard

FOREWORD

She was a new reporter and her first assignment was to interview the local "ghost author" for a Halloween feature. Being new, she was eager and excited to pursue her task. I, on the other hand, was somewhat less enthusiastic.

For anyone who collects and writes ghostlore, the Halloween season is a busy time, with book signings and talks to local groups, as well as a myriad of just such reporters seeking to add some color to their annual Halloween feature. While the attention is of course gratifying, the truth is that by the second or third interview, the average writer begins to develop a sense of what is going to be asked and shifts quickly into "autopilot" mode.

Such was the case in this interview until about ten minutes into our discussion, when she stopped me cold by asking a question I had never been asked before.

"What do you think you give the world through your writing?"

I was dumbfounded. In truth, I had never before even considered the idea that through my simple writing I could be giving something to my readers, much less the world. Surely, when Dickens penned *A Christmas Carol,* he was truly giving the world a gift. When Washington Irving related the adventures of the Headless Horseman, he was giving generations a truly magical contribution. However, the idea that my meager collections of ghost stories might give something to the world seemed presumptuous to the point of arrogance.

I am not sure just how I answered the reporter's question that day, but since then it has stayed with me. What, if anything, do these stories have to give?

As I mull the question over in my mind, I find myself going back to the first time I ever really fell in love with ghost stories. As chronicled in the introduction to my first book, it was sitting around a campfire in my back yard during the last week of summer, listening to my older brother do his level best to ensure that a group of eleven-year-old boys would not sleep that night. In this, I think he nearly succeeded.

For me, that was a night of wonder and magic. Sitting before the light of that backyard campfire, I was transported to a realm of imagination, where the "rules" of life did not apply and where spirits whispered in the darkness. Far from the morbid, sensational tales that pass for ghost stories today, in the innocence of that dark night I was caught up in the enchantment that ghost stories cast.

Now, of course, I am an adult. Daily I face the realities of life, pay my taxes, and do my best to fulfill my responsibilities. Yet, quite often, I find myself yearning to be eleven years old again, sitting around a campfire and feeling the magic that ghost stories cast around me. I yearn to suspend my modern adult incredulity and be transported to a realm of imagination, where the rules of life may not apply and where spirits whisper in the shadows.

Perhaps, when it is all said and done, this is what I dare to hope my writing provides you, the reader. If nothing else, I hope that I may share with you a campfire around which we can sit together and listen, for a time, to tales of the dead who definitely do not rest in peace and of things that go bump (not to mention screech and groan) in the night, until we have to return to the "real" world.

This is my hope in writing this book. It is my humble wish that these stories would cast their spell around you, as they have around me as I have researched and wrote them.

I hope you enjoy them. Be warned: if it is great parapsychological truth that you seek, then you might well look elsewhere. But if, for just a while, you would like to venture once more into the world where spirits whisper in the shadows and ghosts linger just outside the light of our campfire, then come join me—this campfire is for you.

—MMW November 1, 2000

ACKNOWLEDGMENTS

As I have discovered over the course of my last four books, no writer really works alone. There are truly so many people who deserve my thanks in the writing of this book.

I would like to thank my editor, Loretta Crum, who has shown more patience than I deserved. I also want to thank those who contributed their editorial prowess to this work before it was sent to publishing, Mr. And Mrs. Bill Wilkins, and Mr. Mike Carniello. For all of your hours, skill and help, I am really grateful.

Sincere thanks are due to Chris Woodyard, my dear friend and mentor in the ghost-writing field, for contributing the introduction to this work.

Thanks also to all those who helped with the research of the stories themselves, especially my friends Keith Jones, Troy Taylor, Nicole Jonas, Doug Johns, and many others who contributed their aid.

I owe a deep debt of gratitude to my dear friend and photographer Chris Shultz, who gave of his skill and time to this work.

Special thanks are due to Mrs. Nancy Gray and the staff of Kahler Middle School and the Lake Central School System, as well as the Munster Parks Department for their help and support. Thanks also to Larry and Lee Lavery for their help and advice. A special thank you to Ms. Suzanne Long of the Hammond Public Library for help great help and service.

Thanks (once again) to my oldest friend, Dr. Douglas Zale, for his unflagging belief that I could be a writer, starting long before I believed it myself.

Finally, my gratitude must be expressed to all those who shared their stories with me. I am privileged with your trust, and hope that I did them justice.

Note: In the preparation and research of this book, careful attention has been paid to the retelling of folklore that has, in many instances, been passed down for generations. In the retelling of these tales, at times occurrences have been abridged and rearranged with regard to chronology. Therefore, all reports should be taken as folklore and may not reflect exact historical events.

Additionally, in some cases those who have reported their experiences have asked that their names be changed to protect their privacy. In these cases, an asterisk (*) has been added to their name the first time it appears.

1
THE HISTORIC (HAUNTED) KASKE HOME
Munster, Indiana[1]

"He talked and as he talked wallpaper came alive; Suddenly ghosts walked..."

—*Mark Van Doren, **The Story Teller***

Ridge Road, which stretches from Gary to the Illinois state line, looks today like many urban roadways that extend across the face of northwestern Indiana. Driving west from Gary along this busy thoroughfare, one is confronted with a nearly unbroken panorama of strip malls, gas stations and other vestiges of modern suburban life.

However, as Ridge Road passes through the town of Munster, one comes upon an unexpected and striking remnant of a bygone age. On the south side of Ridge Road, surrounded by picturesque woods, sits the beautiful turn-of-the-century home known to the community as the Kaske House.

Operated as a historical museum by the town of Munster (through its parks department) and the Munster Historical Society, the Kaske House is a valuable and important vestige of northern Indiana history. Charmingly out of place in the hectic pace of the modern world that surrounds it, this lovely old home is a quaint reminder of what life was once like in the Calumet region, long before the advent of fast food restaurants and parking lots.

To tell the story of the Kaske house and the property on which it stands (known to the community as Heritage Park) is to tell the history of this entire portion of northern Indiana. It was here, at what is now the intersection of Ridge Road and Columbia Avenue that the settlement of this portion of northwestern Indiana was begun.

The story of this region actually begins thousands of years before human habitation of the area. The natural geographic ridge from which Ridge Road takes its name was formed over fourteen thousand years ago by the same unique geological forces that formed much of the landscape of northern Indiana. Over eleven thousand years ago, a portion of what is today the Calumet region formed part of the Calumet shoreline of the glacial Lake Michigan.

When the end of the glacial period came, the waters receded, leaving sandy marshes covered with thick vegetation to the south and the Calumet River floodplain to the north. Between there lay a stretch of land that would later serve as a natural highway through the region. This path, which would serve as an Indian trail for thousands of years before the advent of white settlers, is today known as Ridge Road.

In the early 1800s, northern Indiana still remained as a basically untouched wilderness. To the west and north lay the young settlement of Chicago, already showing signs of becoming a great city, and to the south lay vast prairies and thick forests stretching past the young community of Crown Point and nearly as far as Indianapolis. However, northwestern Indiana was still a lush, uninhabited wilderness.

In the 1830s, the first travelers passing through the area en route to Chicago noted a bewildering variety of plant and animal life, including wild turkeys, deer, prairie chickens, and quail. Through the rivers coursed crystal-clear water and in them swam an abundance of otter, pike and rock bass. This rustic region flourished with the natural beauty that once was the Midwest.

So striking was the splendor of the region that Harry Eenigenburg, who was born in the wilds of the Calumet region, later recalled it as "The most beautiful country in the middle-west, with all its streams, high sand ridges, meadows and marshes…"

Perhaps it was the beauty of the area that first attracted David Gibson to the region in the late 1830s as one of its first white settlers.

At the time the only other pioneers were a few farmers who had purchased land to the south. However, unlike his fellow settlers, Gibson, evidently somewhat of a visionary in the realm of business, saw the thickly wooded land adjacent to the sandy ridge (which was becoming an popular thoroughfare for travelers) as an ideal location for an inn.

In about 1837, Gibson built the first structure in what is today Munster. Little is currently known of the small log inn except its general location. However, despite the increasing flow of travelers moving through the area, "Gibson's Inn" could not have been a great financial succes,s for just a few short years later, in 1840, Gibson sold his property and inn to Ira Dibble. In about 1845, the property again was sold, this time to Allen and Julia Brass. This enterprising couple, who had recently moved to Indiana from New York, would make the business a commercial success.

Within a year of purchasing the inn and the two hundred acres surrounding it, the Brasses tore down the Gibson Inn and, using its timbers, built a much larger and comparatively more opulent tavern and hotel over a sound limestone foundation. The new inn was rectangular in shape with a kitchen, two large living rooms, and six bedrooms upstairs.

Business was good, but in 1864, Brass decided to move his family to Chicago and sold his inn to Johann and Wilhelmina Stallbohm. Stallbohm, whose family had recently emigrated from Germany, continued to run the hostelry, offering room and board to the weary travelers who arrived daily by stagecoach. A typical menu of the time would offer guests a choice of pork, quail, pheasant or prairie chicken, all for the price of twenty-five cents. An additional fifty cents would purchase a warm bed for the night.

A year after John and Wilhelmina moved to their new home, their eighth child, a daughter named Wilhelmina, was born. Later in life, Wilhelmina would write fondly of growing up in the gracious and lively inn. Writing in 1934, Wilhelmina would recall:

"It was an important center of life in a community which stretched from Hobart and Crown Point to Hohman House (in North Hammond).

In the early days, we used to have ten or twelve guests every night and it was the stopping place for general refreshment for many daytime travelers.

"In spite of our seeming isolation, the tavern was a busy, thriving place, where life would never grow dull. When I was a child the tavern was the social hall [for the community], where infrequent but well attended dances drew crowds from great distances."

In the years that followed, the tavern continued to be a social, commercial, and political center for the community. In the mid 1860s, a telegraph station was established in the inn, making it the only source of news for the Calumet region. It was through the auspices of this telegraph that the news spread to the local residents of the assassination of Abraham Lincoln in April 1865.

During the years of the inn's prosperity, the Stallbohm family also added improvements to the inn, including the large barn that still stands on the property. This barn was used to store crops from the Stallbohm farm, as well as produce purchased from local farmers to help feed the increasing number of guests.

As gracious and hospitable proprietors, the Stallbohms hosted many of the most learned and influential people of the day. It is said that author Carl Sandburg was a frequent guest at the inn, and George Washington Carver is believed to have visited at least once.

Still, with the passage of time and changes in travel patterns in the area, business began to decline, and in the early 1890s the Stallbohms closed the tavern for good. Johann and his wife continued to live in the building until their deaths in 1899 and 1901 respectively. At that time, the house came into the possession of the daughter, Wilhelmina, who had married Hugo Kaske and moved to Minneapolis some years earlier. In 1905 the Kaskes returned to northern Indiana to make the old inn their home.

By 1907, the small settlement that had formed in large part around a rustic inn had grown into a bustling community, and the town of Munster was officially chartered. However, within two years of its birth, the town would be deprived of the landmark that had given it birth.

On October 31, 1909, an annual Halloween party was held at the venerable old building. By 9:00 P.M., when all but one of the guests and family had retired for the evening, a fire erupted in a first floor addition. The residents of the home were roused from their rest and all escaped, but the inn that had stood graciously along Ridge Road for more than seventy years was reduced to ashes. Only a few pieces of furniture were saved from the inferno, including the piano that had served as the entertainment for the inn.

The next spring, saddened but undaunted, the Kaskes hired two local men, the Kooy brothers, to build them a new home. The new house stood slightly south and west of the inn location, just adjacent to the barn. Though considerably smaller than the inn, the two-story home, with a kitchen and living room on the main floor and four bedrooms on the second floor, promised to provide a warm and pleasant home for Hugo and Wilhemina.

By all accounts the Kaskes were happy and prosperous in their new home. Active socially, politically, and professionally, both Hugo and Wilhelmina were prominent fixtures in the community. The home itself resisted the ravages of time and, though some additions were made, it remained basically untouched through the years, a beautiful and graceful reminder of what it had once been.

In 1949, Wilhelmina Kaske peacefully passed away in her second-floor bedroom of the home where she had lived for so many years. With the death of such a well-known citizen, the local paper publicly lamented the "passing of a woman who has been a stalwart of our community for many years."

The words rang true enough at the time. However, in light of subsequent events, some might well wonder if Wilhelmina has ever truly "passed" from the home and community that she loved so well.

With Wilhelmina's death, the home went into the possession of her daughter, Helen Bieker, and her husband, Lawrence. An educator by profession, Mrs. Bieker continued her parents' legacy of community service by teaching at Hammond Technical High School and the University of Chicago, as well as serving on the first board of directors of the Save the Dunes Foundation. The Biekers, resisting the onslaught of commercial development, continued to preserve and protect the historic treasure of their home.

In 1986, Mrs. Bieker found a way to ensure that the home and land that had been in her family for so many years would be preserved for future generations. The home and wooded acreage were sold to the town of Munster with one proviso: that she would be allowed to live in the home for the remainder of her life. Accordingly, when Helen peacefully passed into death in 1988, the home and its upkeep reverted to the town of Munster.

In order to effectively preserve this historic treasure, the Munster Parks Department immediately developed a committee to study what should be done with the property. With the help of the recently reorganized Munster Historical Society, the town then undertook an effort to renovate the house and nineteenth-century barn, and to convert the surrounding woods into a community park.

Today the grounds have become Heritage Park, with walking trails and a beautiful gazebo. This lovely setting is the site for numerous community events each year and is a common location for picnickers and those wishing to simply enjoy a peaceful afternoon. The gracious Kaske home is open to the public as a museum under the sponsorship of the Munster Historical Society.

While most of the furnishings of the home were sold prior to the town's taking ownership, many period antiques fill the home with the genial atmosphere that has been present there for almost a hundred years. Visitors to the site are treated to knowledgable guides who recount the history of the home and area, making the past seemingly come alive. Wandering through the home today, it is easy to become enraptured with the trappings of a bygone era that surround you.

However, if one listens to the stories that are told by some who work in or have visited the Kaske home, there may well be more history in the home than meets the eye. The historic antiques and period furnishings that fill the home may not be the only trappings of the past that remain. For, as some believe, it may well be that the spirits of some who had given their love to the place remain there after their mortal lives have passed.

One person who believes spirits of the past have remained in the home is Cindy Watson, who is a past president of the Munster Historical Society. An affable, lively woman in conversation, Mrs. Watson easily slips into an engaging history of the home she now works to preserve and of the lives of those who once resided there. Through her work with the Historical Society, Mrs. Watson has been active in the preservation of the Kaske home since the town of Munster took possession of it in 1986. In fact, it was on one of her first visits to the home that she first had a hint that something otherworldly might linger on the property.

"In about 1988, just after the death of Helen Bieker, her executor held a red tag sale on the contents of the home," Mrs. Watson recalls. "The Historical Society volunteered to help with the sale and so I came along. When I first got here, I went upstairs to look around and when I went into that first bedroom, which I later found out had been Wilhelmina's bedroom, I felt...funny. I guess I just felt like something was still lingering there. But, of course, you don't say anything about those kinds of feelings so I just went about my business of helping out with the sale."

However, as it would turn out, Mrs. Watson was not the only one to feel this presence. Cindy relates that at the end of the sale, as workers were cleaning things up from the day, she happened to speak with the secretary to the executor of the estate, who had been present during the sale to collect the proceeds. As the two chatted, the secretary turned to Cindy and remarked, "Boy, you can sure feel old Wilhelmina Stallbohm in that first bedroom, can't you? She's still there!" Almost as relieved by the fact that someone had shared her experience as she was startled by the statement, Mrs. Watson replied, "Yes, she does still seem to be here." "So," she concludes simply, "I was not the only one who felt it. And that was that."

As events were to proceed, however, this was not the end of Mrs. Watson's unusual experiences in the house. As she became more involved with the restoration effort, she began to notice other strange events in and around the home. Actually, it was much more than a feeling that Cindy experienced a few years later while parking her car on the property.

"It was 1995, " Cindy recalls with a touch of warmth in her voice, "and I was coming to the house to meet with the superintendent of parks and the lady who was then president of the Historical Society.

My son, who was about five at the time, was in the car with me and I remember we were running late. It was supposed to be a noon meeting, but it was already past that as I pulled up to the property."

Turning off Columbia Avenue, Mrs. Watson drove up the wooded drive and parked her car next to the old barn that sits behind the home.

"I pulled up to the barn," she says, "and parked within about ten feet of it. The west doors were open and as I parked the car, I happened to look up and saw someone lean out of the barn and look at me for a second and then go back in the barn. It was very fast, but I distinctly saw the figure of someone with gray hair peering at me for just a second and then they were gone."

Thinking it curious that someone would be in the old barn, Mrs. Watson retrieved her son from the car and the two entered the structure, only to find it apparently empty. "There was no one inside at all," she says, "and no way anyone could have gotten out. The east doors were locked from the outside and I know that no one had gotten out past me."

Now thinking perhaps she had been the victim of a practical joke, Mrs. Watson walked to the front of the property where her friends stood waiting for her and immediately asked, "OK, who is hiding in

Photo: Chris Schultz

The Kaske House in Munster, Indiana.

the barn?" Seemingly taken aback, the pair asked Cindy what she meant, and when she explained to them what she had seen, they assured her that there was no on one the property but them.

As strange as this occurrence might seem, its conclusion came several months after the event. "After I saw the figure, I did not talk or think about it much," Cindy says, "until some time later when I happened to be looking though a family album of the Stallbohm family. I saw a picture of Wilhelmina as she was in her mid-fifties and I knew exactly who I had seen that day. Her hair was identical. That sounds strange to say, but I have been a hairdresser for years and I know hairstyles, so I positively knew who it was that I had seen in the barn."

The next encounter with the spirit of the Kaske home did not actually happen to Mrs. Watson, yet she was clearly able to observe its aftermath.

"It was during the renovations after the Parks Department took the house," she says. We were redoing the upstairs and had hired a local painting contractor to paint over some of the old, faded wallpaper. I pulled up one afternoon to see how things were going and found the Parks Supervisor standing in the yard with the painter. He was covered in paint and his eyes were big as saucers. He was plainly scared of something. As soon as I got out of the car, the Parks Supervisor turned to me and said, 'Do you know anything about this place being haunted?' "

"I laughed," says Cindy, "but I could see they did not find it humorous. The Parks guy said, 'No, we are serious. Have you ever seen anything or heard about anything ghostly going on here?' I told them yes, that I had seen something down by the barn, at which time the painter said, 'I quit. I am not coming back here!' and proceeded to get into his truck to leave."

Following the worker to his truck, Mrs. Watson convinced him to at least tell her what had happened. He then told her of an occurrence that was unsettling, to say the least.

According to Cindy, the painter told her that he had been working that afternoon in the upstairs hallway adjacent to the front bedroom. Entering the front bedroom, he had carefully poured paint from the can into his paint tray and then went into the hallway to paint over the wallpaper. As he began to apply the first strokes, however, he found himself suddenly covered in paint as the can inexplicably flew from the room and drenched him.

"He said to me, 'THAT'S IT!' and drove off," says Cindy. "So I came into the house, all by myself and walked upstairs. Sure enough, in the hallway I found this big pool of paint all over the floor. I could not help but laugh and I looked into the bedroom and said out loud, 'Wilhelmina, you can't do this. You have to let go!' I guess she did not want him to paint over her wallpaper."

Mrs. Watson is not the only person to recall this incident. While the painter in question has left the area, his employer does recall the frightened workman recounting the tale to him. "He did not work for me too long after that," the contractor says. "That workman left the area fairly quickly."

Other workers and volunteers also have had experiences at the Kaske home that have caused them question whether the presence of Wilhelmina may have chosen to remain in the house she loved so well. Reportedly, teenage park maintenance workers sent to mow the grass at the property during the summer came back to the park office to complain about "a white haired lady" who stared at them from the front bedroom on the second floor. Wilhelmina, perhaps, was looking over the care of the home that is still hers.

Visitors to the home sometimes admit to feeling a presence in the house, particularly on the landing at the top of the stairs and in Wilhelmina's bedroom. One worker claimed to have consistently felt a cold spot on the landing of the stairs to the second floor, immediately outside of the front bedroom. Others report hearing footsteps and, curiously, several report hearing loud crashes in the home. Invariably, when the area from where the sound originated is searched, nothing is found amiss and no source for the explosive sound can be found.

One fascinating tale came from another painter at the site who was hired to paint the exterior of the windows. Reportedly, the worker came to a parks supervisor and asked if a radio had been left on in the house. Since the house was empty at the time and no radio had been brought in, the supervisor said no and then asked him why he would ask. The painter then reported repeatedly hearing piano music coming from the living room section of the house while he was outside working.

Cindy Watson points out that one of the only original pieces from the home to be saved from the fire at the Inn was an antique piano, which had stood in the living room of the house. A prized possession of the Kaske family, it had given them hours of enjoyment in the days before television and radio, after serving as the only entertainment at the inn for many years. However, at the time the painter reported hearing the piano playing in the living room, the piano itself was in the Munster Town Hall, having been moved there to await renovations at the Kaske Residence.

One person who has encountered such strange phenomena more than once is Brian Kresge*, who was a parks supervisor for several years. During his tenure in that position, he oversaw most of the renovations in the home and therefore found himself in the home a great many times, often alone. As he now recalls, "Sometimes I would see some strange shadows…that I could not explain away. They were nothing that I would get really frightened over, but I could not explain them, either. Then there were other times when I would go through the house shutting all the doors securely and then lock up the house, only to come back the next day to find one of the doors opened."

Some of the more startling episodes encountered by Mr. Kresge and others at the home, however, did not seem to center on the ghost of Wilhelmina, but instead suggests a second presence in the house—that of a child.

Interestingly, stories of a child's spirit in the home, while scattered, have been rumored for many years. As far as can be ascertained, they began with a nurse who was brought in to stay in the home while Helen Bieker was in her last illness.

The nurse later told several people at the time of being awakened one morning at about 5:00 A.M. by a little girl who came into her room and tapped her on the shoulder, cheerfully calling, "Get up! It's time to get up!" Then the child playfully skipped her way out of the room and was gone. So befuddled was the nurse by this unceremonious awakening that it was several moments before she realized no small child was in the home. A search of the house later showed no one fitting the description was indeed present within its walls.

While this story might be viewed as curious, other experiences in the home tend to lend credence to the idea that a child's spirit walks there. One such incident was reported by Brian Kresge and occurred one morning several months after the Parks Department had taken possession of the home. Renovations were in full swing and the house was nearly empty of furnishings, most having been shipped to alternate locations during the work.

On the morning in question, Mr. Kresge arrived at the house early to open it for workers. He had been alone at the home till late in the afternoon the day prior and then had carefully locked the house up before leaving. Now, unlocking the door, Mr. Kresge went inside to wait for the workmen to arrive. As he stepped into the living room area, however, something caught his eye that seemed out of place— something that should not have been there. Sitting in the middle of the floor was a curtain covering a small object beneath. Incredulously, Mr. Kresge bent over and lifted the curtain to reveal a child's small porcelain doll.

Mr. Kresge quickly realized that two things about this happening were particularly odd. This first was that he had never seen the doll in question before. Later investigation revealed that it had not been included on any inventory lists for the home. The second peculiar aspect to the incident was the doll's appearance. Brian Kresge knew that when he had locked up the house the previous afternoon, the doll was nowhere to be seen. However, the next morning it was found in the middle of the living room floor, wrapped in an old curtain, despite the fact that the house had been shut and locked in the interim.

Strange as this occurrence was, there is a yet more enigmatic conclusion to the story. After examining the antique doll that morning, Mr. Kresge carefully rewrapped it in the shroud-like curtain and left it on the living room floor where he had found it. He then returned to the Parks Department office and asked his fellow employees if anyone had been in the Kaske house the previous evening.

When all denied entering the premises, Kresge then described his find of that morning and offered to bring the figurine in to show his colleagues. However, by the time he returned the next morning to collect his prize, it was gone. Workmen in the home denied having seen the doll, much less taken it. The doll had vanished as mysteriously as it had appeared.

Curiously, no identity for the child's spirit may be conjectured. A review of the history of the house does not indicate a child ever dying in the home, although it is possible that such a death might not have been recorded. In the woods that still stand to the east of the home, there is a small cemetery that contains the graves of at least three of the Stallbohm children whose names cannot be found in the family records. In truth, the exact identity of whatever young spirit is said to walk the floors of the home will never be truly ascertained, yet the stories persist.

Other stories survive as well. While the spirit of Wilhelmina Stallbohm and the unidentified child spirit walk the halls of the Kaske home, other spirits seem to do their rambling in the wooded grounds of Heritage Park that surrounds it.

One such story came from a local policeman who parked in the driveway late one night to do paperwork, and who is said to have gotten out and chased a hazy figure that ran across the beams of his headlights. When pursued, the figure seemed to vanish into thin air. Other tales tell of a spectral Indian who had been seen on the grounds. According to Cindy Watson, this sighting made no sense to historians on the site until records were later found that indicated that a Native American had indeed worked as a handyman on the property for Mr. Stallbohm until his death and burial somewhere on the grounds.

If the ghostly handyman does prowl the grounds, then he may have spectral company, for other spirits too are said to walk there. Mrs. Watson says she has heard the story of a ghostly couple who have been felt and seen near the gazebo. Like the others spirits on the grounds, this spectral pair is neither frightening nor menacing, but instead affectionate and seemingly in love.

And so the stories are told that surround this venerable old home and the land on which it sits—tales of phantoms from the past, who linger on in this beautiful estate, perhaps not willing to leave their pastoral surroundings. These are not the mournful phantoms some-times associated with common folklore, nor are they the bloody specters of Hollywood fame. The tales told of Heritage Park and the Kaske home are those of serene, gentle spirits. From the shade of Wilhelmina Kaske who is said to maintain a loving, watchful eye on the home that was hers for many years, to the playful spirit of a child, to whoever or whatever might prowl the grounds at night, these seem to be as congenial and amiable a group of apparitions as one could wish to find haunting an old building.

It is, perhaps, their influence that pervades the atmosphere of this lovely historic landmark. Never menacing or frightening, it is a gentle aura of bygone grace and gentility. Like the whiff of a flower's fragrance on a spring day, it is there and then gone, leaving in its wake the wondering memory of its passage in the hallways of time and the annals of Indiana ghostlore.

2
THE SPIRITS OF WYANDOTTE CAVE
Leavenworth, Indiana[2]

"The Phantom slowly, gravely, silently approached...Scrooge bent down upon his knees, for in the very air through which this Spirit moved it seemed to scatter gloom and mystery."

—Charles Dickens, ***A Christmas Carol"***

There is something undeniably eerie about being in the recesses of a cave. It is ironic that so "earthly" a place might evoke such feelings, yet there is something in the damp chill and utter darkness pervasive there that is reminiscent of the ancient descriptions of the underworld.

Regardless of such a macabre connection, there is also much beauty and wonder in the vast subterranean caverns that dot the United States. Mammoth Cave in Kentucky has been called one of the "Great Wonders of the World," and each year it is visited by millions of tourists and spelunkers (cave enthusiasts) alike. Other commercial caves across the United States enjoy similar popularity, beckoning to the natural human fascination with these vast, mysterious underground chambers.

What many in Indiana may not recognize, however, is that our state has several impressive caves within its boundaries as well. One of the most spectacular is Wyandotte Cave, located in southeastern Indiana, near the town of Leavenworth.

The history of Wyandotte Cave is a rich one. The first people to discover the cave were Native Americans who explored it and began to mine its rich natural resources. Radiocarbon dating of the earliest Indian artifacts found in the cave suggest that Native Americans were present in the cave as long ago as three thousand years. It seems that their main interest there was in mining the minerals chert and aragonite. These were used to fashion jewelry and ceremonial objects, which were then traded throughout the central portion of the continent. In addition, Native Americans also extracted the vast deposits of Epsom salts in order to utilize their medicinal properties.

The name of the first white man to discover the cave has been lost to time. The first written description can be found in 1798, but it is thought that explorers to the region may have known of its existence prior to that time. One tradition suggests that the first explorer to reach the cave was Frances Ignatius Bentley, who allegedly engraved his name on the wall of the cave in 1801. What is known with certainty is that Territorial Governor (and future U.S. President) William Henry Harrison visited Wyandotte Cave in 1806 and also adorned a wall with his signature. Harrison later reported being amazed at the beauty of the cave as well as by the huge deposits of minerals found there.

In 1810, the cave and land around it were purchased by Levi Brashear of Nelson County, Kentucky, who intended to mine the cave for its supply of Epsom salts, as well as saltpeter and gypsum. Despite the fact that his efforts were hampered by a lack of available water, which was needed to leach the minerals from the cave soil, saltpeter from the cave was used to produce gunpowder for American forces in the War of 1812.

After the war had ended, Wyandotte Cave was sold to Dr. Benjamin Adams of Louisville, Kentucky. However, his plans for commercial mining of the minerals found there met with little success and in 1818 Dr. Adams relinquished his rights to the cave.

In 1848, the cave was acquired by Henry Rothrock, a wealthy local landowner who seems to have been more interested in the surrounding land than in the cave itself. Wyandotte Cave might have remained as little more than a local curiosity had not two renowned cave explorers, Norman Coleman and Harvey Link, stumbled across it in 1850. Obtaining the services of Andrew Rothrock, the eleven-year-old son of owner Henry, the pair explored the cave at some length, viewing such now famous formations as "The Pillar of the Constitution" and "Odd Fellows Hall."

Furthermore, after following a slight movement of air detected by their candle flame, the party dug an entrance into a new and heretofore unknown section of the cave which would come to be called the "New Cave." Here they found more wonders, including "Monument Mountain," a vast chamber filled at one end with a spectacular 120-foot-tall pile of broken rock. As they later related, they were also treated to the sight of other large rooms, as well as huge gypsum "flowers" and a small stream with colorless fish and large white crayfish.

Most impressed with what they saw, the pair returned to their homes and began to tell and write of the wonders that they had seen in Wyandotte Cave. The pair even speculated that the cave might be larger than the by-then-famous Mammoth Caves. Soon the public took notice of Wyandotte Cave and tourists began to flock to the area. By 1851, the cave was opened to tourists for a fee, becoming only the fourth commercial cave in the United States. Throughout the succeeding years, as further excavations were undertaken in the cave, guides and explorers discovered several new passages and sections. The discovery of the third level of the cave in 1858 served to redouble the tourist trade.

By 1864, the enterprising Henry Rothrock had opened a hotel on the grounds and Wyandotte Cave had become big business. Cave guides were employed and regularly scheduled tours were conducted. Business continued to boom, with new rooms and passages continuing to be discovered. With the death of Henry Rothrock, the cave passed into the hands of his family, who continued to own and operate it until October 1966, when the cave, along with 1,100 acres of land, were sold to the state of Indiana for $350,000.

The state instituted further improvements, adding electric lights and enlarging passageways. Today Wyandotte Cave is considered one of the premier show caves in the United States. Visitors to Wyandotte Cave are treated to a comfortable journey deep inside the Indiana countryside. Far from the simplistic and sometimes dangerous methods of exploration employed by the early cave explorers, tourists travel down well-lit and well-hewn pathways through the vast subterranean passages, viewing the splendor and wonder of the geological curiosities found there. Still, even with the advent of modern lighting and the ease of travel in the cave, one cannot help but be taken with the deathly stillness of the surroundings and the seemingly impenetrable darkness that hovers just beyond the illumination of the electric lights. Despite the modern improvements made to the cave, the imagination of the traveler might still be struck with the impression of descending into the dark underworld described by the ancients.

Indeed, this disquieting thought might be eerily accurate if the stories told within the dark recesses of Wyandotte Caves are to be believed.

Not one but two very different ghost stories are told to explain the spectral presence said to inhabit the dark recesses of the cave. Both date back to the middle part of the nineteenth century, around the time when owner Henry Rothrock opened the cave to public inspection. Today, the tales are recounted primarily by cave guides such as Luke Stroud, a long time employee whose versions of these tales are recounted here.

The first strange tale told of the cave is known to guides and local folklorists simply as "The Counterfeiter's Ghost." According to the legend, at the time Henry Rothrock was attempting to hire several part-time workers to dig trenches in the cave in order to allow visitors to walk, rather than crawl through some of the tight passages. However, despite the fact that all Rothrock required for the job were a few healthy men with strong backs, at first he is said to have been unable to locate suitable workers. Perhaps many of the able bodied men of the area were already employed, or perhaps the prospect of spending long hours in the dark, closed confines of the cave was not appealing to many young locals.

After a few weeks of posting notices in the area advertising the work available, Rothrock finally received a visit from three men ready to take the job. Strangers to the area, the men explained that they were willing to do the work required provided they could work only late at night. When pressed as to the reason for these hours, the men were evasive in their answers. Finally, although puzzled by this strange request, Rothrock agreed, as long as the excavations could be done well and on schedule.

Over the next several weeks, Rothrock journeyed into the cave several times to check on the work being accomplished and was gratified to see the project apparently progressing well. However, due to the unusual hours being worked, Rothrock did not see his employees except on Friday mornings when they would walk from the cave after a night's work to collect their weekly pay. All seemed to be going well with the arrangement until another Rothrock employee made a strange discovery.

The employee in question, a tour guide at the cave, was taking time from his duties to explore on his own. As he tramped through one of the small passages in the lower section of the cave, where no one was regularly allowed, the guide discovered a large, heavy crate. Puzzled as to why such a large box might be there deep inside the recesses of the cave, the man immediately left and went to the home of Henry Rothrock to report his finding.

Later that day, Mr. Rothrock himself journeyed into the cave to examine the strange crate. After carefully inspecting the box, he opened the lid and was shocked to find a small printing press and engraved plates which clearly indicated that what he was examining was a counterfeiting machine. Scrutinizing the plates, Rothrock suddenly understood the nature of his late night employees.

Working late at night to avoid detection, the men were using Wyandotte Cave as a base of operation for producing counterfeit U.S. currency. With this realization, a jolt of fear shot through Rothrock. Clearly, should this illegal activity be discovered by authorities, it would immediately be assumed that he was a part of this criminal endeavor, perhaps even its ringleader. With the prospect of prosecution and jail before him, Henry Rothrock decided he must immediately alert local police to his discovery. By bringing forth the information himself, he could avoid any chance of being implicated in the crime.

That afternoon, Rothrock saddled his horse and rode to nearby Leavenworth, Indiana, to share the news of his discovery with the local sheriff. Although initially skeptical that counterfeiters would be operating in rural Indiana, the sheriff did agree to return with Rothrock in order to examine the box himself. Together the pair rode back to Wyandotte Cave.

After examining the contents of the box, any doubts the sheriff held were vanquished completely. Clearly, they now had to capture the counterfeiters. After a hasty consultation, a plan was agreed upon. The next morning being Friday, it was decided to capture the criminals when the three workers came to collect their pay. As they emerged from the mouth of the cave, where Rothrock would customarily meet them, they would be ambushed and quickly apprehended.

The next morning, just as dawn was painting the eastern sky, all was set. As Rothrock and the sheriff stood just outside the cave, a team of deputies crouched on a ledge directly overhead, waiting to pounce on the men from above. At the appointed time, the figures of the three workers emerged from the mouth of the cave, unaware of the trap that was awaiting them.

However, at the last moment something went wrong with the ambush. As the trio walked into the bright morning light, the deputies jumped a moment too soon. Two of the criminals were immediately captured but the third, a few steps behind his friends, was missed. Realizing what was occurring, the man turned and quickly sprinted back into the darkness of the cave.

After hastily securing the first two criminals and lighting torches, the sheriff and several deputies pursued the fleeing criminal. At first guided by the sound of footsteps echoing from the caverns before them, the group moved swiftly forward through the maze of passages, until they arrived at the "Mountain Room." Here the party was greeted with nothing by silence and a huge pile of broken rock devoid of human presence. The culprit had disappeared.

Thinking at first that the man had doubled back on them, making his way back to the cave entrance, the posse retraced their steps, but upon arriving at the mouth of the cave they were assured by the deputies waiting there that the man had not been seen. Now sure that the criminal was trapped in the cave, the sheriff decided that it was best to wait him out.

Instead of searching for him in a dark cave that was still largely uncharted, the sheriff decided to post a guard at the entrance of the cave and wait for him to give himself up. Without food or water, the criminal surely could not last long in the cave.

As days turned to weeks, the guards kept careful watch at the entrance without result. Day and night, law enforcement officials maintained their vigil, yet the man never appeared. After three weeks had passed, it was decided that the man must have died somewhere in the cave and the guards were removed. It was even speculated that perhaps, trying to climb the heap of fallen rock in the Mountain Room, he might have inadvertently caused a minor avalanche, burying himself alive. In any case, no trace of him has ever been found to this day. However, some suggest his presence has been felt in the cave ever since that time.

For, from that time on, those visiting the Mountain Room have reported seeing the shadowy shape of a man walking among the rocks. Today, when tour groups enter that area of the cave, guides customarily turn off the lights and light lanterns to give participants a feeling for what cave exploration was like before the advent of electric lighting. On more than one occasion, tourists have reported seeing, in the flickering lantern light, the outline of a man wandering along the perimeter of the room, as though searching for a way out.

Others, including tour guide Luke Stroud, have had additional experiences in the cave that might indicate a ghostly presence there.

"I was walking down some stairs in the big room," Stroud recalls. "I was going there with a friend to change some lights and as I walked down the stairs, I noticed to my left a cloud of dust that moved down the stairs right beside us. It was great big person-sized. It was a large, billowing kind of form that moved right with us. We did not hear anything fall to create the dust, but there it was following us." Stroud goes on to note that since the area is well underground, a breeze in the area capable of stirring up a dust cloud of that size is practically impossible.

Others have reported hearing strange voices from within the cave. One story even has a guide running through the cave late one afternoon chasing the sound of a person calling for help. As he moved through the dark passages, the voice seemed to change locations, luring him deeper and deeper into the bowels of the cave. At last giving up his chase, the guide returned to the Visitor's Center to report a lost tourist, only to find that no one had been in the cave all day. Perhaps, as some have speculated, it was the voice of the long-lost counterfeiter, pleading for assistance in finally finding a way out of his eternal imprisonment in Wyandotte Cave.

As evocative as the story of the Counterfeiter's Ghost might be, it is not the only ghost tale told of Wyandotte Cave. If, as some believe, the ghost of the doomed counterfeiter does indeed wander its vast subterranean passageways, searching for an exit he has never found, then perhaps he has company in his rambles—another spirit, more diminutive and innocent. Herein lies the tale of Andrew.

The tale of Andrew Rothrock can be traced to the 1850s, during the early days of exploration. About that time, the vast expanse of the lower caves had been discovered and Henry Rothrock, as well as a host of others, was busy investigating and mapping the new sections of the cave. Among those who maintained an avid interest in exploring this previously unknown area was Andrew, the eleven-year-old son of Henry Rothrock. Though still very young, Andrew was both daring and skilled at cave exploration.

As his exploration of the lower section continued, it became apparent that Andrew knew that part of the cave better than any adult of the area and he was frequently used as a guide for other explorers. Such guidance was vitally important, because at the time the descent into the lower sections of the cave could prove dangerous to anyone who was not well acquainted with the passageways. If not carefully guided, a novice explorer could easily become confused in the many twists and turns of the cave and become helplessly lost in the dark.

Such was the predicament of two young men a few years after the discovery of the lower cave. According to the legend, two hunters returning from a long and fruitless day in search of game found themselves tramping by the mouth of Wyandotte Cave on their way home. On a whim, one of the young men suggested that it might be fun to enter the cave and do a little exploring, in order to add some adventure to an otherwise disappointing day. Both were local men who had explored the cave before, so the plan seemed like a good one.

Because they had been hiking since before daylight, both carried small lanterns which they produced and lit. Then, hiding their rifles in some brush beside the entrance, they began their exploration. After traveling back some distance into the cave, they came to a formation known today as the "auger hole," a small opening that descends into the lower section of the cave. Squeezing through this tight passage, the men entered the third level of the cave, an area into which neither had ever ventured before.

Continuing their aimless wandering, the men had walked nearly a mile into the third level when one of the men, stumbling on a rock formation, dropped his lantern and shattered it on the floor of the cave. Undaunted, the intrepid pair continued on with their walk, using their lone remaining lantern for illumination. Eventually, some two miles into the caverns, they began to hear the sound of water falling to their left. Following the sound, the pair rounded a curve in the passageway and entered a room known as Milroy's Temple, a large chamber with a flowing waterfall along the far edge. Here the young man bearing the lantern laid it on the floor, allowing him and his companion to step back and admire the beauty of the room. It was a nearly fatal mistake.

As the pair stood, swept away with the majesty of their surroundings, neither realized that the lantern had been laid directly below a stalactite formation on the roof of the cave. It was a drop of water, dripping from this formation that fell onto the wick of the lantern below, extinguishing its flame and plunging the hapless hunters into total darkness. In desperation, one of the young men fumbled for his packet of matches and lit one, only to have it flare for a moment and then go out. After several unsuccessful attempts, the young man succeeded in lighting his sole remaining match and managed to put it to the wick of the lantern, but the wick, still wet, extinguished the flame. Once more the hunters were left in total, impenetrable darkness.

Finally, now, the gravity of their situation fully dawned on the men. Without a light, finding their way back to the entrance of the cave was unthinkable. Since no one was aware of their presence in the cave, it seemed unlikely that a rescue party would be dispatched unless their guns were somehow discovered in the underbrush at the cave entrance. Furthermore, although some water was available to them from the waterfall, they carried with them only a little food. Indeed, their sole hope lay in staying where they were and hoping against hope for a miraculous rescue.

For three days the pair lay in absolute darkness, the days and nights slowly melting together. By the third day, both men had given up hope. On the morning of their third day of captivity in the cave, one of the men had wept himself into an uneasy slumber, while his companion lay with his eyes open to the utter darkness surrounding him. As he silently prayed, however, suddenly something in the distance caught his attention. It was a faint light, the first that he had seen in three long days. Scarcely able to believe what he was seeing and wondering if perhaps he was beginning to hallucinate due to hunger and fatigue, the man watched as the glow came ever closer.

When the light was close enough to begin to illuminate his surroundings, the hunter let out with a hoarse yell, rousing his friend from sleep. In a moment, through the passageway to their right the men saw the figure of a small boy emerge. Later, reflecting on the events as they had transpired, both of the men would note that they never saw the lantern the boy was carrying for light. Instead, the child seemed to be cloaked in a warm light that almost blinded the two men due to their time in the darkness.

However, at that moment the men did not think to wonder at the source of the light brought by the child. Instead, they simply watched, wide-eyed, as the boy walked a few steps toward them and casually inquired, "Can I help you?" Rising to his feet, one of the hunters shouted out a grateful "yes," and then explained that he and his partner had been lost for days in the cave. "OK," the boy replied. "Follow me and I can get you out."

Joyfully the men grabbed their packs and followed as the boy led them back through the passageways of the cave, always keeping a little ahead of them yet close enough to allow his light to guide them. When, at long last, the men saw daylight streaming from the entrance of the cave before them, both men ran past the boy and out into the freedom of the outside world. After screaming for joy and hugging each other for a moment, the pair turned to thank the boy who had been their salvation, but he had already turned away and was disappearing back into the darkness of the cave.

Thinking that they would return the next day to find the young boy and thank him, the pair returned to a joyous reunion with their families. The next morning, true to their resolution, they returned to the cave bearing presents for the boy to express their thanks. Finding no one at the cave itself, the hunters made their way to the nearby home of the Rothrock family and knocked at the door. When it was opened a moment later, Henry Rothrock greeted them and invited them inside.

Haltingly, the two young men told Rothrock of their perilous adventure in his cave and of their rescue at the hands of a young boy. However, when they asked if Rothrock might know who the boy had been, the gentleman shook his head and said that no young boy would have been in the caves the day before. The episode they were describing, he said, was impossible.

At this, the two men broke into a chorus of protests, saying that they knew what they had seen. It was only when one of the young men described the child that a strange and questioning look crossed the face of Henry Rothrock. He stared at the floor for a moment and shook his head and then looked back at the two men again. "Wait here for a moment" he said gravely. "There is something I want to show you." With these words, Henry Rothrock walked out of the room. In a moment he returned carrying a small picture. Showing it to the two puzzled men, he asked, "Is this by any chance the boy you saw yesterday?" "Yes!" came the exclamation from the men. "That is the boy! We want to thank him—where is he?"

A look of shock and disbelief passed over the older man's face and then after a moment, he seemed to soften. In a voice cracked with emotion he said, "I'm afraid you will not be able to thank him—at least not in person. This is a picture of my son Andrew. Please, gentlemen, have a seat. I think I should tell you a story."

Sensing something ominous, the two men placed themselves on the chairs offered by Rothrock and sat in silence for a moment as he stared down at the photograph, seemingly lost in thought. Finally he looked up, his eyes glimmering with tears. "Yes," he said, his voice choked with emotion, "this is Andrew. I guess I should not be surprised he could get you out—but what you are saying is still impossible.

"Andrew loved the cave," he continued slowly. "Every day after school, as soon as his homework was done, he would be off exploring. We really did not worry about him down there because he knew those caverns better than anyone did. It was like a second home to him..." Again Rothrock's voice trailed into silence.

After a moment, one of the young men broke the awkward silence to say "Look, sir, we just came to thank the boy. If he is not here we can come back later." "That will not be necessary," Rothrock said flatly, looking directly at the man. "You see, a couple of years ago, we started to notice that Andrew had a cough. It was not bad at first but then it got worse. We decided that he was catching a cold from the damp of the cave and we tried to keep him out, but he loved the place so much that he would sneak off to it when we were not looking.

"Of course, we took him to all the local doctors, but they could find nothing wrong. Then my wife decided to take him to a hospital in Indianapolis to one of the doctors there. The doctor said he had something called Histo Plasmosis. It is a disease of the lungs that you get from being around bat droppings, like in caves. He didn't give us much hope—just told us to keep the boy quiet and to keep him out of the cave.

"We did just as the doctor said," Rothrock went on, the tears now streaming down his face. "We took him home and put him to bed— kept him away from the cave, but it did no good. His cough kept on getting worse and all the time he kept on asking if he could just go back into the cave one more time. At the end of it, we could tell that he did not have much time left and so I gave in. We wrapped him in blankets and I carried him into the cave one more time. We went down to the Mountain Room and I propped him up against the wall there so that he could see the cavern. I remember he said to me 'This is such a beautiful place—I wish that I would never have to leave it.' I could not think of what to say in return and so I just reached out to hold his hand but when I did, it was already cold and limp."

Scarcely unable to believe what they were hearing, one of the hunters broke from his trance and asked, "What are you telling us sir?" Snapping back to full attention, Rothrock peered at the men directly and in voice choked with emotion replied, "I am telling you my boy died in the cave. We buried him there the next day. That was a year ago yesterday."

As Rothrock stared once more at the floor, wrapped in his paralyzing grief, the men sat before him in stunned silence in the wake of their inescapable surmise.

Caves, one of the more earthly of all possible places, do indeed have a distinctly unearthly quality to them. There is something in the utter darkness and hushed silence that brings to mind visions of the underworld pictured by the ancients. And, perhaps, within the precincts of Wyandotte Cave of Indiana, this picture may be more telling than one might think. Here within these silent walls, the dead are said to linger. Perhaps it is the spirit of a fugitive from the law, searching for an exit he has never found. Perhaps it is the innocent spirit of a young boy who returns to be of help to those in need.

Whatever the case, if you happen to find yourself walking through the wonders of Wyandotte Cave in southern Indiana, do not be surprised if you hear the hushed passing of an unseen traveler along those well-worn passageways, or even glimpse a dim shadow that should not be present. Do not be alarmed. It is just the spirits of the cave, seeking the companionship of the living for a brief moment before they part company—one of you returning to the land of light and sunshine and one to eternal habitation in the blackness of the caves below. They are an inexplicable part of the darkness in that subterranean domain.

3
THE PROPHET'S GHOST
AND OTHER SPIRITS OF TIPPECANOE
Battlefield, Indiana[3]

"I see dead people...some of them scare me. They can't see each other. Some of them don't know they're dead. They tell me stories... things that happened to them...things that happened to people they know. They're everywhere...You won't tell anyone my secret, right?"

—*Haley Joel Osment,* **Sixth Sense**

They were two men, both leaders of their people, whose lives and fates took them in very different directions. One would be destined for honor and glory and one for defeat, disgrace, and ultimately, an anonymous grave. They were two men whose lives were set on a collision course, while in the balance hung the hopes of their respective nations. It was a fateful collision that would take place on the bloody fields of an area that is even today known as "Battlefield."

Today, the beautiful fields of Battlefield, Indiana, lie in pastoral serenity. On spring mornings, the mist clings close to the lush green countryside, obscuring the forms of deer and rabbits that come to peacefully feed, a tranquil scene that belies the bloody and violent history of the site. For it was upon this ground, almost two hundred years ago, that two great nations and two important leaders came into violent conflict. It was a clash that would play a key role in the sealing the fate of their respective peoples.

The Battle of Tippecanoe is the single most important battle ever fought in the state of Indiana. Though comparatively minor in terms of duration and number of combatants, it would play a pivotal role in the future of western expansion in America, as well as sealing the eventual fate of the Native American tribes of the Midwest. It was a clash of two warring nations, a clash of cultures, and a clash between the two men commanding their respective armies.

Interestingly, both of these men led lives that were at once very different, yet strangely parallel. Both were born to important families to their nations, both felt the call of political and military leadership, and ultimately both would meet untimely deaths. Both felt a keen desire to protect their nations from the encroachment of the other. They met but once—on the bloody battlefield called Tippecanoe, and there their place in history was forged.

William Henry Harrison, then governor of the Indiana Territory and future president of the United States, could boast of purely American lineage. Born on February 9, 1773, at the Virginia plantation known as Berkley, Harrison was the seventh child of an already august political family. His father, Benjamin Harrison, was a signer of the Declaration of Independence and a close friend and political ally of George Washington.

Born to both the privilege and duty of colonial aristocracy from an early age, Harrison was instilled with the values of leadership and service. Though he felt a keen interest in a military career, it was the intention of Benjamin Harrison that his youngest son would be a doctor. Accordingly, after an early education at home, William left Berkley to attend Virginia's Hampden-Sidney College and then went on to study medicine in Richmond and Philadelphia. While Harrison was a bright student, his heart did not seem to be in his studies or his prospective career. With the death of his father in 1791, William promptly left school to enlist in the still-neophyte American army.

So it was that William, at age eighteen, found himself thrust into the conflict that was simmering in the Northwest Territory. As a newly commissioned ensign in the First Regiment of Infantry, Harrison was stationed at Fort Washington, near what is today Cincinnati, Ohio. It was here that William received his baptism by fire, fighting skirmishes with the Indian tribes that were resisting American intrusion into their lands. Despite his age and inexperience, Harrison distinguished himself as a brave and able soldier, and when in 1792 General Anthony Wayne assumed command of troops on the Western frontier, he was sufficiently impressed with Harrison to promote him to second lieutenant and have him assigned as his personal aide-de-camp.

In 1794, Harrison was cited for bravery at the battle of Fallen Timbers, and when the treaty of Greenville was signed in 1795, temporarily ending hostilities between Native Americans and settlers, Harrison was promoted to captain and placed in command of Fort Washington. It was there that Harrison married and started a family that would ultimately number ten children.

Despite his meteoric rise through the army ranks, Harrison soon became frustrated with the meager wages afforded an army officer and resigned his commission in 1798. However, his personal fortunes continued to rise when he was immediately appointed by President John Adams (an old friend of his father) to the position of secretary of the Northwest Territory. The following year, he was elected as this territory's first delegate to Congress.

In 1800, Harrison returned to the area as the first appointed gover-

Photo: Chris Schultz

"Prophet's Rock," where the Prophet is said to have watched the battle of Tippecanoe.

nor of the Indiana Territory, which consisted of much of what is today Indiana, Illinois, Wisconsin, Michigan and Minnesota. His was a daunting task. Officially, it was his duty to establish an effective government in the wilderness region, to keep the peace, and to ensure the welfare of the growing stream of American settlers coming to the area.

More problematically, as governor it was Harrison's responsibility to deal with relations between settlers and Native Americans. This proved to be a monumental task because the flood of new pioneers to the territory brought increased tensions between the two peoples, especially with regard to land.

In 1802, the administration of President Thomas Jefferson authorized Harrison to negotiate treaties with the various Indian tribes in the area with the aim of annexing of their lands while maintaining their friendship. The two parts of his instructions would ultimately prove incompatible.

As a negotiator with the Indians, Harrison proved to be determined and shrewd. During his twelve years as governor, Harrison would convince the native peoples to sign treaties giving up nearly all of their lands in the territory. In one treaty alone, signed at Fort Wayne in 1809, Shawnee leaders were convinced to forfeit their claims to nearly three million acres.

Understandably, not all Native Americans were pleased with the prospect of giving up their hunting lands and homes. With the passage of time, an increasing number of Indian leaders foresaw the end of their control of the territory and thus their way of life. Even before the treaty of Fort Wayne, a few scattered Indian bands initiated action against the American setters in Indiana.

The hostility began simply enough. Horses were stolen from remote farms in the region. Lone pioneers were ambushed and killed as they rode the wooded trails of the area. As time passed, these attacks became more frequent and the Native American warriors bolder. However, at least during the early years of Harrison's administration, the Indian resistance still was scattered and disorganized. Unless the Indians could become unified in their struggle, they held no real hope of holding their land and stemming the tide of American intrusion. Leaders were needed who could unite the diverse Indian tribes into a common front. As fate would decree, two such leaders were about to appear—two men whose destinies were tied to one another as well as to that of their white enemy, William Henry Harrison.

The Indian Chief Tecumseh, was born in 1768 in the Native American settlement of Old Piqua near present-day Springfield, Illinois. His brother, Lauliwasikau, was born ten years later. The two boys grew up in a family of eight children under the tutelage of their father, Puckeshinwa, a great Shawnee chief. As a result of this influence, Tecumseh and Lauliwasikau were groomed as leaders in their tribe from an early age. The elder, Tecumseh, seemed to bear this responsibility with a quiet nobility, quickly acquiring the reputation as a fearless warrior and a wise leader, adept at council and strategy.

Lauliwasikau, however, seemed less able to bear the weight of the responsibility thrust upon his shoulders. Smaller and less proficient at the skills of hunting and warfare so essential to Indian braves, he was quickly overshadowed by his older brother. This was further exacerbated by several events that occurred in his early life.

As a young man, Lauliwasikau lost an eye to an accident with an arrow. This necessitated his wearing the black eye patch that would become his brand for the rest of his life. While today such an attribute might be treated merely as an unfortunate handicap, in Indian society it was considered a mark of shame.

As Lauliwasikau grew, his ostracism from his family and tribe grew. He was regarded as lazy, and as a young man he discovered the wiles of the alcohol brought to the region by the white man. He quickly became addicted to the "firewater," further diminishing his status among his people.

Meanwhile, Tecumseh was earning the respect and leadership of his people. Significantly, as a young man he was sent by his father as an emissary to other tribes in the Midwest in order to make peace or settle disputes over hunting land. During these diplomatic trips, Tecumseh had the opportunity to hear from other tribes news of the white man's new incursions into the area and to share the growing frustration felt by most Native Americans at the time.

By 1807, Tecumseh, by then the chief of his tribe, saw the situation growing worse. The treaties being signed by Harrison and representatives of other tribes in the area were quickly depriving the Native Americans of their hunting land and homes. Further, the steady stream of settlers to the area was becoming a flood, and Tecumseh saw dark days ahead for his people unless drastic measures were taken. Quietly, he began to prepare for war.

In 1809, Indian leaders were called to Fort Wayne to negotiate a treaty that would ultimately take most of the Indiana territory from their hands. Whereas the forceful and eloquent Harrison awed most of the Indian representatives present, Tecumseh was appalled by what he saw as the stealing of the land from his people. In the end, he rejected the treaty and publicly condemned those chiefs who signed it.

It can be said that Tecumseh clearly saw what the other chiefs present did not. Tecumseh knew that neither the treaty about to be signed nor any that might follow would satisfy the need of the white men for land. Yet, he was also shrewd enough to understand that none of the tribes present in the territory, operating on their own, was strong enough to defeat the usurpers. However, if the diverse tribes could somehow be unified, combining their strength and numbers, then perhaps in time the settlers could be driven from the land.

Now Tecumseh saw his life's work before him. Utilizing the skill he had acquired in dealing with other tribes as a young man, he would become an ambassador for confederation among the Indian nations throughout the Midwest and South. It would be through his visionary leadership that his people would come together to once and for all defeat the white man.

In these seemingly grandiose plans, Tecumseh found an unlikely aid and ally—his brother, Lauliwasikau, who had by then risen to the status of medicine man among his people. Having conquered his youthful battle with alcohol, in 1805 Lauliwasikau announced to his people that he had received a vision from the Great Spirit. In this vision, it had been revealed to him that, if the people would give up the ways of the white man that they had been slowly adopting (including the use of alcohol) and return to their ancient traditions, they would achieve victory and drive the usurpers from the land.

The people responded by proclaiming Lauliwasikau a medicine man. Accordingly, he adopted a new name for which he would become famous: "The Prophet."

Together, Tecumseh and the Prophet became an effective team in uniting their people. While the elder brother excelled as a statesman and politician, the younger brother gave a mystic vision and hope to their dispirited people. Beginning in 1808, the two began to slowly work toward a united Indian confederacy.

With characteristic political vision, Tecumseh quickly decided that a capital for this confederacy was needed. Together, he and his brother traveled to the confluence of the Wabash and Tippecanoe rivers near what is today Lafayette, Indiana, and established a village known to the whites as Tippecanoe and to the Indians as Prophetstown. This would serve as a central meeting place for the various tribes that would agree to federation, as well as a training ground for the emerging Native American force. During the following years, the two brothers worked unceasingly to form the military and political alliances necessary to defeat Harrison and American forces in the area.

Ever the statesman, Tecumseh was frequently absent from the village, going as emissary to tribes as far removed as Georgia and seeking their aid in the common cause. In his absence, the Prophet ruled the village, encouraging the increasing number of warriors in the camp and delivering frequent visions from the spirit world. Characteristically, these visions promised victory against the white men if they would remain true and vigilant to their cause. At its peak, as many as a thousand warriors lived and trained at Prophetstown, preparing for the battle all knew would come.

By the winter of 1811, white settlers had become fearful of the ominous presence of such a large contingent of armed Indians in their midst. While formal assurances were still being sent from the Prophet to the territorial government that their intentions were peaceful, most knew that hostility was not far away. By that summer, William Henry Harrison had received permission from Washington to begin raising an army to counter the Indian threat and had amassed a militia of roughly a thousand men.

That fall Tecumseh left his brother at Prophetstown in order to meet with Indian tribes in the middle west and southern United States. If he could enlist the aid of the mighty Apache and Sioux nations, then surely the success of his ultimate mission would be ensured. Leaving the Prophet in Indiana with approximately 800 to 1,000 warriors, Tecumseh reportedly warned his brother not to make war with the white men under any circumstances until he returned in a few months with more reinforcements. In all probability, these instructions were due to two factors. First, the warriors that Tecumseh hoped to return with would give them the numerical strength needed to effectively defeat Harrison's army. Secondly, Tecumseh knew that his mystical brother lacked the proper military sense to wage an effective campaign. In any case, it was advice that would be fatally ignored.

In November of that year, Harrison realized that Tecumseh was gone from the village and sensed an opportunity to at least disperse the warriors assembled there. He moved toward Prophetstown with his militia. On November 6 they arrived within a few miles of the settlement and a contingent of soldiers was sent to parley with representatives of the Prophet. In a few hours, the detachment returned to Harrison with assurances that there would be no hostile actions from the Indians until a meeting could be arranged the next day. The Prophet had also indicated his assent to the militia force moving forward toward the village to camp for the night. That day, the forces under Harrison marched toward the Prophetstown, camping on a high ridge just a mile or so from the village.

Many have since wondered why the Prophet chose to provoke a battle with Harrison's forces early the next morning. Some credit a "mystic vision" that he claimed to have received. Some believe that he was legitimately convinced that Harrison's men would attack during the night, necessitating his men to strike first. Others suggest that he was hoping to prove himself as a military leader, thus finally escaping his brother's shadow. In the end, we will never know.

What is known is that late that evening, the Prophet called his chief warriors to a council. There he announced that the Great Spirit had revealed to him that it was Harrison's intention to attack and wipe out the village early the next morning. He then said that the way to achieve victory was to attack at first light, wiping out the troops in a surprise attack. He further stated that that as long as he was their chief and would chant his medicine song during the battle, the bullets of the white men would pass through the warriors without harming them. All that long night, the war drums beat as the braves danced around their council fires.

Shortly before dawn, the Indian force crept silently forward toward Harrison's camp. As had been arranged, the Prophet took his place of command on a large outcropping of rock overlooking the battlefield, from which he would direct the battle and chant his song of power. Meanwhile, his forward scouts crept to within a few hundred yards of their enemy and waited until dawn when they would shout the attack.

Their waiting was actually cut short when, just before dawn, Harrison ordered his regimental drummer to sound wake up call to the men. The Indian scouts, crouched in the darkness a short distance away, heard the sound of the drumming and, believing it to be a signal of attack, set up a cry for their own forces to strike.

The Indian warriors were upon the soldiers before most militiamen knew what was happening. In the opening moments of the battle, it seemed as though the territorial forces would be routed as Indian warriors swept through the outlying encampment, shooting and clubbing bewildered soldiers just rising from their sleep. Some historians have since speculated that, since few of the militiamen had any prior battle experience, many may have broke from their stations and ran.

As dawn slowly warmed the eastern sky, no doubt the Prophet looked down from his perch on Prophet's Rock and felt the thrill of approaching victory.

Victory, however, was not to be his that day. The Indian advance stalled as Harrison's soldiers began to hear the alarm and take their place in the reformed battle line. Several waves of Indian warriors were repulsed as they attempted to break through the American lines, and then, shortly after dawn, a counterattack was organized that began to repulse the Native Americans.

Meanwhile, the Prophet sat on his rocky perch, his arms outstretched, his voice lifted in a chant. A runner was sent to him bearing the message that, despite his assurances, his braves were indeed fall-

THE PROPHET'S GHOST   37

ing in increasing numbers to the militia bullets, but the Prophet refused to call for a retreat. Instead, he ordered his forces to continue their fight to what he promised was a victorious conclusion.

By late morning, the forces under General Harrison had the situation well in hand, and the Indians were in full retreat across the battlefield, leaving many of their number lying dead or wounded in the grass behind them. The battle had lasted only slightly over two hours and the militia casualties were counted as 62 dead and 126 wounded. While no count was made as to the casualties among the Native American forces, it was clearly seen that their spirit was crushed.

Their confidence in their leader gone, the Native American forces came face to face with the fact that their hopes of a victory were dashed. Later that day, the Indian forces abandoned the village of Prophetstown, leaving most of their supplies and belongings behind. The Prophet, who just a day earlier had been heralded as their great leader, was taken in bonds as a prisoner to their next encampment.

When Harrison's army moved into the village on November 8, all they found was an aged woman, whom they removed and then reduced the encampment to ashes. Then the army began their march back to Vincennes.

While, in military terms, the battle of Tippecanoe cannot be considered on the same scale as many of the major battles fought in the history of the Western Conquest, its significance for all concerned cannot be overestimated. For the Indians, it meant the end of any real hope of a confederation against the Americans. While many tribes would continue to offer scattered resistance against the white men over the next several years, never again would they provide a united front. Most returned to their tribes and villages disillusioned, their dream of a united Indian nation shattered on the bloody fields of Tippecanoe.

Significantly, in addition to drastically affecting the fate of the nations involved, the battle of Tippecanoe set the fates of the major leaders in the conflict. While he was not at the battle itself, Tecumseh, upon his return, found his people scattered and dispirited and his hopes for an Indian confederation obliterated. While he would continue his struggle against American forces for several more years, eventually fighting for the English in the War of 1812, he would never again attempt to rebuild his coalition. He was killed in the Battle of Thames on October 5, 1813, at age forty-five.

The Prophet, who found his status falling from medicine man to prisoner in less than twenty-four hours, fared no better. With the return of his brother three months after the battle, the Prophet was exiled, shunned by the very people he had once hoped to lead to victory. He went on to Canada for a few years before returning to Ohio in 1826. A short time later, he was forced to relocate with other Shawnee to a settlement west of the Mississippi. He died in an Indian settlement in Kansas in 1837, still despised and rejected by his people.

Contrary to the fate of his two opponents, the future hopes of William Henry Harrison seemed to rise significantly after the battle of Tippecanoe. Parlaying his success against the Indians into political fame, Harrison was elected Senator in 1825 and then was elected president of the United States in 1840 under the slogan, "Tippecanoe and Tyler too." His political and personal fortunes seemed at their zenith.

However, even this greatest success was to elude Harrison. Just two weeks after his inauguration in March 1841, Harrison developed pneumonia and died on April 4. His one-month tenure as president was the shortest in American history. At the time of his death, at least one pundit put forth the theory that his demise was caused by "the curse of Tecumseh, visiting retribution on him for his humiliation of the Indian Peoples."

While such a supposition might well be considered as sensationalistic hype, throughout the succeeding years there have been hints that other repercussions of the battle of Tippecanoe have continued—repercussions that have filtered down through the passing decades like ripples in a pond, until they reach out in strange and uncanny ways to effect the lives of those in the present day.

Beth Scott and Michael Norman, the acknowledged deans of Midwestern ghostlore, recorded one such story in their book, *Historic Haunted America*. According to Scott and Norman, the residents of a farmhouse in Warren County, which lies along the path taken by Harrison's army over a century ago, have reported strange occurrences. Frequently, on cold nights in early November, they have reported being awakened by a strange sound resounding through the night air.

In the distance, the sounds of a martial drum have been heard, beating a march cadence. Then, faintly at first and then becoming clearer, come the resounding hoof beats of horses and the rhythm of tramping feet, as though a military procession was passing close by the farm. Though the residents have looked out into the night to see the road in front of their home empty, the sounds continue for several minutes and then recede into the distance. Though no concrete explanation may be made for these sounds, the residents reported to Scott and Norman that they believed this was the ghostly army of William Henry Harrison, marching forward toward a phantom battle with the spirits of their Indian foes.

If this supposition is true, it would partially explain other rumors that have continued for generations in the area of the battleground itself—rumors that have been passed from father to son, neighbor to neighbor, hints that the battle of Tippecanoe might not be as finished as history has recorded.

One such tale comes from Jerry Derrick, who grew up in the area of the battleground. Derrick, who is today a computer consultant in northwest Indiana, vividly remembers his years spent in the rolling countryside of battleground.

"When I was a kid and especially in high school, I spent a lot of time on the battlefield," Derrick now says. "A few friends and I would go out there as little kids. It was the perfect place to play cowboys and Indians. Then, when we got into high school, we would sometimes picnic out at the park or even sneak out there after dark just to roam around—I guess it was just the ordinary crazy adolescent thing to do." It was on one of these covert nighttime rambles that Mr. Derrick and his friends experienced something distinctly out of the ordinary.

"I remember it was sometime in early November," he says, "because it was just getting cold at night. I was probably a senior in high school and a couple of my buddies and I drove over to the battlefield one Saturday night. I'm not sure, but I think maybe one of the guys had stole a couple of beers from his parents' refrigerator and we were going to be cool and drink them, but if so, then we never had the chance."

As Jerry now recalls, the friends parked their car on a nearby road and then walked onto the battlefield grounds, sitting on a hillside overlooking what had once been the field of combat. "We were laughing and cutting up and the talk turned to the battle. One of my friends said he wondered if there were any dead Indians buried in the field. I said that there probably was and then we just forgot about it. However, about a minute later I noticed that it suddenly had gotten considerably colder. There was a breeze that just came out of nowhere and it was stirring the trees around us. I remember that I said something about how cold it was getting and was just putting the hood of my jacket up when we heard the sound of chanting."

As Mr. Derrick now relates, the sound seemed to be muffled, as though coming from a distance. "At first we did not know what was making the sound, but then it began to rise and fall with a regular cadence and as it got louder, we could hear the sound of a number of voices chanting, almost like it was a song. Then it got a little clearer still, as though it was getting closer and we could hear the sound of tom-toms beating along with the rhythm of the chant.

"I have been accused of many things," Jerry says, a wry smile crossing his face, "but being overly brave was never one of them. One of my friends said to me 'Who's is making that sound?' and I just said, 'I don't know, but I'm sure as hell not going to stick around and find out. Let's get out of here!' "

With these words, the boys all rose and turned toward the area where their car was parked, but in a moment their progress was halted by a sound that stopped them in their tracks. "It was a war cry," Jerry remembers. "It sounded right next to where we were standing. Not in front of us, or behind us, but it sounded like it came from exactly where we were standing. Yet the moon was out and we could see no one was around.

"Needless to say, we cut and ran like the devil back to my friend's car. Just before we jumped in, one of my friends looked back toward the field and swore that he saw a figure on horseback watching us from a distance. I did not see anything, but I was too busy nosediving into the back seat to look around."

In the subsequent years, Jerry and his friends have discussed their common experience several times and all remember it vividly. "It seems like it was just yesterday," Jerry concludes. "The experience is burned into my memory, primarily because I had never been as scared as I was that night and I am grateful to say that I have not been that scared since."

As traumatic as their experience was to Jerry and his adolescent friends, a still more extraordinary tale of the battlefield is told by Carl Lisek*, a civil engineer who now lives a short distance from Battlefield, in West Lafayette. The tale is one which his father, Bill, told him many years ago. As Carl recalls the story today, his eyes seem to sparkle with the same sense of excited awe the story must have generated in him when he first heard it from his father nearly forty years ago.

"You have to understand that my dad was a very truthful man," Carl begins. "He was not one prone to exaggerate anything and he would be the last person on earth to make up a story or tell a lie. So when he told us that he had seen the battle of Tippecanoe being re-fought, we had to believe him."

According to Lisek, his father, a maintenance manager at Purdue University, drove the road that wound past the battlefield almost daily for over forty years, often late at night or early in the morning. "My dad was in charge of maintenance for three of the dormitories at Purdue and a lot of times when a boiler would go out or something, he would get called out in the middle of the night. This was more or less a regular occurrence so he was used to driving by the old battlefield at all hours."

While returning from one of these late night trips, according to the tale he would later tell his sons, Bill Lisek saw a scene out of time and reason on the battlefield of Tippecanoe. "According to what my dad later told me," Carl recounts, "he was driving along the road that abuts the park early one spring morning just as the sun was coming up. He told my brother and me that it was a beautiful morning and as he looked over at the field, he saw that the fog was lying close to the ground, giving it almost a surreal look."

It was then, according to Bill Lisek, as he drove down the road with the first rays of dawn painting the eastern horizon, that he began to notice something distinctly odd. As he later told his sons, he noticed at first one, then many, shapes moving through the fog that shrouded the field before him. "Dad said he looked and he could see figures moving around in the mist, and then he saw the forms of riders on horseback," Carl says.

Unsure of just what he was witnessing, Lisek quickly pulled his car over to the shoulder of the road and peered into the fog. As the first rays of the sun continued to evaporate the hovering fog, a bizarre spectacle unfolded before his unbelieving eyes.

"My dad swore to us that he saw the whole battle going on right in front of him," Carl Lisek says. "He saw Indians swarming forward, some on horseback, with old-time rifles and tomahawks and soldiers in strange-looking uniforms shooting back at them. This was not some dream or vision—my dad said it looked very real except that there was no sound—it was like watching a silent movie only in 3-D."

Unable to believe his eyes, Bill Lisek at first thought that some sort of historical reenactment might be taking place, but this thought quickly passed from his mind as he saw Indians shot from their horses, blood spraying from their wounds. Soldiers on the ground broke from their positions and ran, only to be clubbed to the ground by their pursuers. No historical reenactment could ever portray such appalling reality.

Then, abruptly, the vision passed. "My dad told us that he was not sure just how long the battle in front of him lasted," Carl says. "He said that it could have been a few seconds or it could have been ten minutes—he could not tell, but then, suddenly, it was gone and my dad was left sitting there in his car, unable to believe what he had seen."

It was not until many years later that Bill Lisek, reading for the first time a history of the battle of Tippecanoe, realized that the timing of his vision, coming just after dawn, corresponded almost exactly with that of the actual battle. Still, such a confirmation did nothing to provide a logical explanation for what he had witnessed. However, in the years to come he would tell his children and grandchildren of the strange sight he had seen on the fields of battleground.

"In the end, I cannot explain what my dad saw any more than he could," Carl Lisek says. "All I can say with certainty is that he believed he had seen it. If you could have heard him tell the story, you would understand just how real this incident was to him."

It should be clearly noted that none of these strange events are chronicled in the official histories kept by the Battleground State Memorial. Indeed, officials at the park say they are unaware of any ghostly tales told of the park.

Yet, in the community surrounding the once bloody battleground, the stories remain, handed down through generations, perhaps enhanced and enlarged with each retelling. A hiker in the park is said to have been unnerved, one day, by the sight of a lone militiaman in costume of long ago, watching him from the edge of the woods.

One another occasion, an elementary school student who had picked up an arrowhead from the battlefield is said to have awakened that night to the strange sight of an Indian brave standing over his bed staring at him. The figure disappeared in an instant, yet when the boy awoke the next morning, the arrowhead was gone from its place on his dresser.

Perhaps the most poignant and telling stories are the recurring tales of a solitary Indian apparition, said to be seen sitting on Prophet's rock, staring intently out towards the fields before him. According to legend, it is the ghost of the Prophet himself, lamenting his fate that was decided so long ago. Perhaps he is mourning a nation and a way of life that was lost on the bloody battlefield of Tippecanoe. And perhaps he awaits a chance to redeem himself from the shame of dishonor the engulfed him over a century ago.

4
THE RESTLESS SPIRITS OF HANNAH HOUSE
Indianapolis, Indiana[4]

"For over all there hung a cloud of fear, a sense of mystery the spirit daunted and said as plain as whisper in the ear, 'This place is haunted.'"
—*Thomas Hood*

Indianapolis, Indiana, has been called "a big city that still feels like a small town." Although it is the state's largest metropolitan area, Indianapolis at times still conveys the wholesome aura of a small Midwestern town. While the city has experienced huge growth in recent years, both industrially and in terms of population, somehow in the midst of this onrush, it seems to maintained some vestige of the small town it once was.

Perhaps the essence of Indianapolis is best summed up by a local resident who puts it this way: "Indianapolis is a place that can offer you all the things that you look for in a big city, but it is also a place where you can still get change for a pay phone from the guy on the street." This dichotomy in nature is apparent throughout the city. A tour of the downtown section reveals some of the best of what a Midwestern city can be, including world-class restaurants, entertainment and sports facilities. Yet, not far from the downtown area, one can find quiet streets where neighbors still sit out on their front porches on summer evenings and children play on sidewalks. Old homes sit back from the street in serene dignity, like the grand dames they are, silently surveying the changes time has wrought around them.

Further, it may be in some of those homes that some remnant of the past lingers on—restless specters who, it is whispered, have chosen, or perhaps somehow have been fated, to remain in the world of the living, long after their mortal remains have been consigned to dust.

One such prominent home is the Hannah House. Built in 1858 by famed Indianapolis philanthropist Alexander Hannah, the home has become well known as a striking example of perfectly preserved nineteenth-century architecture. It has also become known as arguably the most famous haunted house in the state. As such, it has been featured in at least two books detailing famous American haunted houses and has been the subject of a number of local television and newspaper accounts. In short, Hannah House has earned a valued place in Indiana ghostlore as our most famous haunted landmark.

Alexander Hannah was born in Wayne County, Indiana, in 1821. As a young man, he opened a harness-making shop in his hometown, but in 1850 the lure of easy wealth made him forsake his home state for the goldfields of California.

Unlike many Hoosiers who responded to the call of gold, Hannah, primarily through enterprise and hard work, made out well in the ensuing years. While never "striking it rich" in the gold mines, he did earn enough money to purchase an interest in a barley and vegetable ranch in California, which prospered by supplying the needs of the booming population of the state.

After five years of association with the ranch, however, Hannah decided to sell his interest and returned to Indiana, settling near Indianapolis. There, Hannah took a position with the Indiana Central Railroad of which his father, Samuel, was president. Once again, through hard work and ingenuity, Alexander Hannah prospered. In the next several years, Hannah began to purchase some of the vast land holdings in Indianapolis belonging to his father, extending his land to 240 acres by 1857.

In November 1858, Hannah began to collect materials for the construction of what would eventually be one of the most beautiful and ornate homes in the community. Probably inspired by trade publications and architectural digests of the time, Hannah designed a home based on Greek Revival and Italian influences. Using the latest advances in building techniques and the best craftsmen available, Hannah was rewarded for his efforts with a home that was truly a showplace. Built on a "foursquare" plan, the home exuded an atmosphere of quiet gentility and elegance. With its substantial red brick exterior and twenty-four rooms, the mansion provided ample space for the bachelor Hannah and his servants, as well as the many guests who visited the home. During the next several years, many parties and gatherings were held in the home as Hannah continued to ascend in prominence in the community.

During that time, Hannah expanded his interests both professionally and personally. He was known as an innovative farmer, employing the latest advancements in agriculture and agronomy. Hannah also became a generous benefactor in the community, giving liberally to many civic and religious organizations.

Also active in civic life, Alexander Hannah served his young community as sheriff, clerk of the circuit court, and state legislator. He is said to have been a friend and early supporter of Abraham Lincoln and importantly, was known as an ardent abolitionist. Indeed, for many years, tales have persisted that his house was a stop on the Underground Railroad. While (as is the case with most homes used for this purpose) no records exist to substantiate this, the stories would later play an important part in the ghostly tales told of the old mansion.

In 1872, Hannah took on a new and (perhaps due to his age) unexpected rol: that of husband. In that year, Hannah gave up fifty years of bachelorhood when he married Miss Elizabeth Jackson. Perhaps conceding to the wishes of his new bride, in the next year Hannah added a service wing to the back of the home consisting of a summer kitchen, smokehouse, milk house and servants' quarters.

By all accounts, Alexander and Elizabeth Hannah were happy in their home for the span of their years there. Though the couple remained childless, it is believed that they suffered through the stillbirth of a child sometime during their marriage. Despite this loss, the Hannahs shared a comfortable and happy existence in the home until their deaths.

In 1895, Alexander Hannah passed on to his eternal reward. Since his wife had preceded him in death and there were no living heirs, the estate was subdivided and sold. In 1899, the house and twenty-one acres of surrounding land were sold to Roman Oehler, a prominent local jeweler. Upon his death, the house was given to his daughter, Romena Oehler Elder, who in turn passed it to her son David in 1962. After a restoration that lasted from 1981 to 1999, Hannah House is now open to the public for parties, meetings, and banquets.

Despite the changes wrought by time, today Hannah House stands much as it has for nearly one hundred and fifty years, a beautiful and historic landmark. Yet, it could be said that the fame of Hannah House also lies in a more mysterious realm. For with the passing decades, this gracious mansion has also become famous for the ghostly tales told of it.

The best-known legend of Hannah House centers around the popular belief that the house was used as a station on the Underground Railroad during the pre-Civil War period. While, as has been noted, no historical records exist that can verify the fact that the home was used for this purpose, historians indicate that a lack of documentation is common in such instances. By the very nature of the endeavor (illegally hiding runaway slaves) homeowners took pains to make sure that no records were kept that could be used as evidence against them.

Moreover, it does not seem unlikely that Hannah House could have been used to house runaway slaves. Alexander Hannah, a great humanitarian, was outspoken in his views against the cruel institution of slavery. As an ardent supporter of Abraham Lincoln, his heart was clearly with the cause of abolitionism. Finally, the house itself would have been well suited to the job of a clandestine way station for runaway slaves. While today, Hannah House sits squarely in a developed residential area, in the mid 1800s the home was considered remote, surrounded by a huge estate. Thus, no prying eyes could witness mysterious wagons coming and going late and night and unloading their human cargo. Furthermore, due to the expansive size of the home, slaves could be well hidden in case of a visit by authorities.

According to old tales told, Alexander Hannah had a secret room built into the basement to serve as housing for the escaping slaves. Here they would be housed, fed, and cared for for a matter of days or even weeks until the next leg of their journey to Canada could be arranged. Though windowless and dank, owing to the dirt floor, the room provided essential security for those seeking freedom. Here they would huddle in the confinement of their basement sanctuary, dreaming of the day when liberation would become a reality.

However, according to the story, one night while a group of slaves waited in the secret basement room, tragedy struck. The lantern that provided their only light was knocked over and the flames quickly caught the wooden timbers of the room. Because the door to the room had been locked in case of a raid by authorities, the haven of sanctuary for the slaves quickly became a fiery prison. Before Alexander Hannah and members of his household staff could intervene, several of the former slaves had succumbed to the flames and smoke. So as to avoid detection, the dead were quickly buried under the dirt floor of the room. In later years, a cement floor was poured over the area, further entombing the doomed slaves.

While no historical records exist to substantiate this story, tales of the event have been handed down from generation to generation at Hannah House. Moreover, some would argue that this story and the incident that it portrays hves had strange and inexplicable consequences at Hannah House. For many years, those who have lived in and visited the mansion have reported eerie incidents in the basement area. Many have reported a mysterious smell in the room where the slaves are said to have been kept. At least one has described it as the strong odor of sweat and humanity, as might be produced by a great many people crowded into an enclosed area for an extended period of time. Others have reported hearing moans or stifled screams coming from the basement.

One of the most common manifestations that has been noted from the basement is reported by researcher Nicole Jonas, who recently conducted several interviews of people associated with the house. One of those she interviewed was David Elder, the grandson of Roman Oehler, who had purchased the house from the Hannah estate. Mr. Elder has previously lived in the rambling old mansion and now helps to manage it as a business.

Mr. Elder reported to Ms. Jonas that at one point, while he was alone in the home, he heard the unmistakable sound of breaking glass rising sharply from the basement. At the time, he noted, there was a shelf containing rows of unused canning jars standing along the basement wall and it sounded as though each jar in turn was being thrown to the floor and smashed. Thinking perhaps a neighborhood youth had broken into the home and was in the process of vandalizing it, David Elder ran to the basement, only to find the area undisturbed and no broken glass anywhere.

Others have reported similar sounds emanating from the confines of the basement. Richard Winert and Nancy Ishmael, in their book *More Haunted Houses,* interviewed Gladys O'Brian, who lived in the house on and off for ten years in the 1960s and 70s and ran an antique store on the main level of the mansion. Mrs. O'Brian told the authors, "I've heard the sound of crashing glass at least five times. One time, two deputy sheriffs were called in and they both heard the noise." So loud was the sound that Mrs. O'Brian compared it to the sound of a china cabinet being pushed over.

Mr. Winert and Mrs. Ishmeal also quote Gladys's husband, John, as having heard the sound of breaking glass from the basement, In *More Haunted Houses,* he is quoted as telling the authors about one such instance just before he and his wife moved into the house.

"The house was unoccupied at the time. It had been empty for five years. I was downstairs in the main part of the house, tying up some old newspapers, when there was the loud sound of glass breaking. It seemed to come from the basement. I thought maybe someone had broken in and had knocked over a barrel of fruit jars. But when I ran downstairs, no one was there. I guess it was just a matter of hearing something that wasn't real. But it was a very, very loud sound. Of course, it was a rainy, dreary day and you can imagine how a noise like that would add to the spooky atmosphere."

This is not the only time that Mr. O'Brian apparently encountered strange sounds coming from the basement of the mansion. Elsewhere in *More Haunted Houses,* Mr. O'Brian tells of walking in the front door of the house one evening and crossing the entrance hallway. "I took about three steps," he said, "and each time my foot touched the floor, it sounded like somebody was underneath, banging the floorboards with a sledgehammer. That happened many times and my wife experienced it too."

Interestingly, the basement is not the only place where strange incidents seem to occur. Ghostly phenomena have been noted throughout the house. According to Nicole Jonas, residents of the house are said to have distinctly heard footsteps echoing through empty hallways. One resident claimed to have clearly heard a woman's light footsteps pass him on the staircase, noting that the sound resembled that of a high-heeled shoe striking a hardwood step. However, not only was there no one else in the vicinity but, incredibly, the staircase itself had been carpeted in recent years.

According to Michael Norman and Beth Scott, in their classic book *Haunted Heartland,* there also have been sightings of a mysterious man who seems to appear and disappear throughout the house. The book notes that the first sighting of this man seems to have been by Gladys O'Brian, during the time when she and her husband ran their antique business in the home.

One evening, while climbing the stairs to the upper level of the house, Mrs. O'Brian is said to have looked up to see a man in a black suit walk across the hallway in front of her. Thinking that a customer had somehow ventured from the store on the first floor into the closed second floor, Mrs. O'Brian quickly climbed the stairs to locate the intruder, but by the time she reached the top he was nowhere to be seen. By now alarmed, Mrs. O'Brian called her husband and together the pair searched the home but without success.

Norman and Scott also write that Mr. O'Brian later encountered the phantom, this time standing beneath an archway on the stairs. He described the figure as semi-transparent, but distinct enough for him to note that the phantom sported mutton-chop whiskers and was wearing an old-fashioned black suit.

Other things, too, have been heard in the hallway. According to researcher Nicole Jonas, the sounds of rustling clothing have been heard in the hall, as though a woman in the long dress of the last century were passing. In *More Haunted Houses,* Gladys O'Brian reported an even more eerie sound. In the book, Mrs. O'Brian relates that one night when she was in an upstairs bedroom watching TV, her leisure was destroyed by an "ungodly sound" coming from the hallway. "I turned the sound off [on the TV]" she related, "and opened the door to the hall. There was definitely someone or something groaning out there. Then it stopped and I went back to watching TV again. About an hour later, however, it started all over again. So I said out loud 'If I can help you, please tell me. If I can't, go somewhere else and do your bellyaching'. At that, the groaning stopped."

Other eerie things, too, have been known to occur frequently in the house. Locked doors have been known to fly open of their own accord, only to slam shut a moment later. Chills and drafts are felt in closed rooms. According to Richard Winer, John O'Brian witnessed one such occurrence in a distinctly dramatic and inexplicable way.

"We have a door to the attic that will not shut or open unless the handle is turned hard," he says. "One night I heard something in the attic and I ran up there, thinking that I would catch someone playing tricks." As he did so, however, he was shocked when the door handle turned by itself, the door opened and a cool draft of air rushed down at him. A search of the attic later found it to be empty.

Objects have also been known to move of their own volition at Hannah House. Interestingly, at least one of the stories comes from a time in the early 1980s when the Indianapolis Junior Chamber of Commerce used Hannah House for their annual Halloween "haunted house." As such, the home was rigged with spooky tricks and effects meant to scare the paying visitors. However, during the three years the Jaycees used the home, a few of the haunting effects seen were not in their script.

Once, a group of workers, relaxing in the old summer kitchen, were startled to hear a loud scratching sound seeming to come from inside the wall of the staircase landing next to them. David Elder, owner of the home, quickly dashed underneath the stairway to find the cause of the noise, but none could be found.

In their book *Haunted Heartland,* Beth Scott and Michael Norman also interviewed Dick Raash, who was the coordinator of the event for the Jaycees. He told of a time in 1980 when he brought his home stereo unit to the house to reproduce the chilling sounds that would greet visitors to the event. The unit in question had a on/off button that had to be pushed to start or stop the soundtrack.

According to Raash, one evening he and a friend were in the house alone checking out the details of the event (including the soundtrack) when suddenly the music stopped. When the pair returned to the location of the stereo to check the problem, they found that the button had been pressed to turn the machine off.

Puzzled and a bit uneasy, Raash pressed the button once again, starting the eerie soundtrack, and the pair went about their business. However, a short time later the entire sequence of events repeated itself. "Somebody *had* to have pushed that button," Raash told Scott and Norman, "but there was no way someone else could have been in the house."

The authors of *Haunted Heartland* also chronicled another strange event that occurred about the same time. According to the book, in October 1981, a film crew from the Indianapolis television show, "PM Magazine," came to the house to film a Halloween segment. At one point in their tour of the house, a cameraman was setting up his equipment in the dining room doorway, preparing to take a shot. Gazing up at a beautiful antique chandelier that hung in the living room, the cameraman turned to a fellow worker and remarked, "Wouldn't it be eerie if that chandelier moved?"

At that moment, as though on command, the chandelier began to swing back and forth in a six-inch arc. "We stood there with our mouths open," commented one of the seven witnesses to the event. However, as it turned out, the ghosts of Hannah House were not done having fun at the expense of the television crew.

Later in the day, after touring the home with local paranormal investigator Allene Cunningham, the crew was setting up in a room where they would do some final footage. To add atmosphere to the shot, the crew borrowed a coffin that had been brought in for the Jaycee haunted house event and propped it up against the back wall of the room. As the television host stood in front of the coffin, preparing to film the conclusion to the segment, a picture hung on the wall above the coffin suddenly fell and clattered violently to the floor.

As the film crew examined the picture and the wall from which it had fallen, their curiosity turned to cold chills. It was found that the two-inch nail on which the picture had been hanging was still securely nailed into the wall and was in fact still at an upward angle, eliminating any chance that the picture had slipped downward off the nail. Furthermore, the wire attached to the frame of the picture was still sound and intact. To those present there seemed no logical way that the picture could have fallen down, particularly at the moment it did. Perhaps the answer might lie in some real ghosts celebrating Halloween in their own unique way.

Gladys O'Brian, in *More Haunted Houses,* reported another strange instance of an object that seemed to move on its own. She recounted how, in the early 1970s, she hired a painter to work in the house who, in her words, "the house rejected." From the moment he stepped in the door his first day, odd things began to happen. Doors slammed as he walked by. Pictures began to fall off the walls when he was in the vicinity.

The climax of the events came one day when Mrs. O'Brian came to bring the worker coffee. As she related the incident to authors Winer and Ishmael, "I poured the coffee and put the spoon back down on the tray. I turned around for a second and glanced back just in time to see the spoon fly off the tray and hit the wall—all by itself." The frightened painter quit that very day.

An odd sequel to the story came a few days later, after Mrs. O'Brian's son came to finish the job that the painter had so abruptly left. The first night he was alone in the home, the young Mr. O'Brian had the unsettling feeling that he was being closely scrutinized by a presence he could not see. Consequently, the second night, he brought his wife and daughters with him for company as he worked, thinking this might ease his feelings of discomfort. However, this strategy failed when one of his daughters spent a good portion of the evening downstairs in the home talking to an older man that no one else in the family could see. When the child reported that the man was coming up the stairs, apparently to visit her parents on the second level of the house, Mr. O'Brian quit his work for the night and took his family home.

One area of the house that has become noted for strange occurrences is the first bedroom in the upstairs section of the house. According to research by Nicole Jonas, this was the bedroom occupied by Mrs. Oehler during her last illness and death in the early 1900s. Since that time, several inexplicable stories have become attributed to this bedroom. By far the most noted phenomena are the unusual smells that have been encountered there. According to Richard Winer in *More Haunted Houses,* these smells vary dramatically in their nature and intensity. Winer quotes John O'Brian as telling the story of his first encounter with the phantom odors.

"I walked in there one morning," O'Brian related to the author, "and it smelled like something or someone had been dead a long time. I tested the floorboards to see if something could have crawled under there and died, but I did not find a thing. Then, the next instant, the whole atmosphere changed and the room just smelled like a rose garden. I thought there was something wrong with my sense of smell, but my wife also noticed the odor and so did people who have visited and did not know a thing about the house."

Mrs. O'Brian, too, has claimed to have smelled the nauseating odor and told Winer that she had scrubbed the floor with a number of cleaning solvents in order to cleanse the room of its smell, but without success. Despite her best efforts, the smell seems to come and go of its own volition. It is interesting to note that with the passing of time, the recurrence of the smell of death in the room has apparently subsided and today, residents of the house indicate they have never encountered it, although some do admit smelling the more pleasing aroma of roses in the room at odd moments, even in the dead of winter.

It is also perhaps significant that several people who claim to be "sensitive" to ghosts have indicated that they sensed the spirit of a pregnant woman in great pain in the room. Some have indicated that they believe that the woman had given birth to a stillborn child. Until a few years ago, this story was given little credence, since there was no record that a child had ever been born in the house, even a stillborn child.

However, in an effort to shed further light on the story, researchers eventually visited the Hannah family plot at Crown Hill Cemetery in Indianapolis. Between the graves of Alexander and Elizabeth Hannah was a small unmarked gravestone, of the type commonly used for infants. While the discovery proves little conclusively, it might well give the skeptical inquirer cause to wonder.

Indeed, many of the stories attached to this regal old mansion might well make one wonder. From the tales of doomed fugitive slaves ending their mortal live in a basement inferno, to the spirit of a jauntily dressed older gentleman, to whoever or whatever causes the strange smells permeating an upstairs bedroom, the tales of Hannah House swirl about the residence like windblown leaves on a autumn day.

Today Hannah House has been restored to its previous splendor and serves the public as a refined setting for gatherings and banquets. The current residents of the house say that they have noticed few strange incidents of late, which might suggest that the spirits of Hannah House are now at peace, since their beloved home has been elegantly and lovingly restored.

However, few in the area doubt that there may still be some remnants of the past in this beloved local landmark. Whether mischievously knocking pictures from the walls, or gliding silently through the halls of the mansion, perhaps they still linger. If so, then they substantiate the reputation of Hannah House as the most famous haunted house in the state of Indiana and one of the crown jewels of Indiana ghostlore.

5
WHERE NOT ALL THE DEAD REST IN PEACE
A Funeral Home in Southern Indiana[5]

"A house is never silent in the darkness, to those who listen intently; there is a whispering in the distant chambers, an unearthly hand pressed the snib of the window, as the latch rises. Ghosts were created when the first man woke in the night."

—*James Matthew Barrie,* **The Little Minister**

It's just down the way—you know the place…past the old courthouse and down that street with all the tall elm trees. It is that old house the children whisper about as they pass by. Tales of it have been told around dinner tables and campfires in the region for many years. No one can deny that it is a place of the dead. But in this stately house, at least one of the dead does not rest.

When beginning to research ghostly tales, one fact that becomes readily apparent is that ghosts rarely appear where anticipated. Often, in the tales told, specters are found where they are least expected. A brief scan through the annals of Indiana ghostlore reveals stories of ghosts inhabiting such unlikely haunts as a modern hospital, several elementary and high schools and even an airplane hanger—hardly the stereotypical settings for ghostlore.

Conversely, some sites that one would naturally assume to be haunted turn out to be frustratingly unghostly. Not every dark Victorian mansion harbors a host of ghostly denizens, and not every rustic, foreboding cemetery can boast of a legion of resident spirits. Indeed, according to ghost researchers, cemeteries and places naturally associated with the dead are some of the least haunted locations for which to look for ghosts.

According to Troy Taylor, president of the American Ghost Society, "Most places associated with ghosts are places that the spirits were connected with in life. Most people do not spend a lot of time in cemeteries in life, so they will not haunt them after death."

The same could be said of other locations associated with death and dying, most notably funeral homes. While many people experience a sense of unease with funeral homes due to their intimate relationship with the death and sadness, in reality the relationship between funeral homes and those they serve seems to end when the dearly departed vacate the premises. Not many, it seems, desire to stay behind in the location of their last farewell.

However, standing on a quiet street not far from the town square of one small city in southwestern Indiana, there is one funeral home that seems to be an exception to this rule.

A most stately building, Johnson Funeral Home* looks little like the modern, antiseptic buildings common in some of the more recently built funeral homes. Indeed, the funeral parlor looks very much like what it was first built to be—a home. Built in 1910 by local mortician Alvin Johnson*, the house was designed to serve both purposes. The four-story Victorian home, complete with a turrets and ornate latticework, fairly speaks of Old World charm and ambiance. Inside, a marble floor in the entryway leading to oak paneled visitation rooms on either side add to the dignity of the home. To the rear of the main floor, a small office stands next to a staircase, which leads to the family living space on the second floor and a large, open third floor used today for storage.

When Alvin Johnson moved to Indiana from Ohio in 1908, he was twenty-one years old and newly graduated from mortuary school. At the time, the town he moved to was little more than a few dirt streets and a local grocery that doubled as the town's saloon. However, sensing the possibility of future commerce, Johnson put down his roots. In those days, formal funerals were not commonplace in rural Indiana. Most funerals were still conducted in homes, with little preparation for the deceased. Caskets were made from rough-hewn lumber, often knocked together by relatives from whatever spare boards were available.

In such a situation, Johnson set about to show local residents a more dignified way of memorializing their dead. Borrowing funds from his family in the East, Johnson planned the construction of a building that would certainly be the most impressive structure in the rural community. When the building was complete, it stood tall and elegant, seeming oddly out of place amid its rustic surroundings.

In the spring of 1909, Alvin Johnson advertised his new "mortuary" as open for business. During its early years, the business struggled financially and Mr. Johnson was forced to supplement his income from funeral work by using his home as an apothecary and furniture store. Still, as the years passed and the surrounding community continued to develop, the Johnson Funeral Home came into its own.

In 1950 Alvin Johnson turned over the day-to-day operations of the funeral home to his son but continued to live and work there until his death in 1976 at the age of 89. In 1992, his son, Bob Johnson*, sold the business to Dale Kuzemka* who has run the funeral home since that time.

"I know that it sounds strange when you are talking about a funeral home, but I fell in love with the place when I first laid eyes on it," says Kuzemka. "I grew up near Detroit and went to mortuary school in Louisville. After graduation, I went to work at a large funeral home just outside of Indianapolis. It was a good place to start out, but it was a modern funeral home that did a huge business, so we had little personal contact with families. After about two years a friend told me about an old funeral home in a small town that was up for sale, so my wife I and traveled down here one weekend. We loved the small town feeling and we absolutely loved the funeral home and living quarters upstairs. I talked with Mr. Johnson that day and made an offer to buy the business, despite the fact that I did not have any financing to back up the offer."

However, the amiable Mr. Johnson was receptive to Dale's interest and agreed to sell him the business and home on a five-year contract.

He further agreed to work with Mr. Kuzmeka for the first two years of his ownership in order to ensure a smooth transition. "For a young guy just starting out in the business, it was too good to be true," Dale remembers. "And, for me, one of the best parts was working with Bob Johnson. He was a gentle, kind man and he knew everyone in town. He and his father had been here so long that their family was virtually an institution in this town and having him around was a great help in my first couple of years there."

When Dale and Becky Kuzemka first moved to their new town, they took up residence in the second and third floors of the funeral home. "The second and third floors had been the home of the Johnson family from the time that the home was built," Becky now remembers. "But after Alvin Johnson's death, when his son took over the business, he did not live in the funeral home. He already had a house in town and so he didn't move in. So, the second the third floors had been vacant.

"Some of my family thought it was strange at the time," Becky continues with a smile. "They were not too sure when I married a funeral director to begin with, but now, here I was a bride of two years, moving lock stock and barrel into a funeral home. My parents nearly flipped, but I have to say the charm of the house just took me. All things considered, it was a lovely place to live but it was still six months before my parents would come and visit us."

It was while the couple were first moving into their new home that Becky noted a few incidents that, while seeming minor at the time, would later take on an eerie significance to the Kuzemkas.

"The first thing that I remember was really pretty minor," Becky recalls. "It was the first week we were moving in. We did not have many possessions—aside from the few pieces of furniture and a bed, most of our belongings were packed into a couple of cardboard boxes. But one of my treasures was an old Victorian picture that my grand- mother had given me. It had hung in the living room of her house for many years and after we got married, she had given it to me.

"The first day we moved in, I found a place in our living room and hung it over the mantle. But the next morning when I got up I found the picture on the floor. What was strange was that the hook was still in the wall where I had screwed it in the day before. So, I hung it back up and went back to the job of moving in. But later that afternoon, after lunch, I found it on the floor again."

Thinking that perhaps vibrations in the wall were shaking the picture off the hook, Becky then asked Dale to provide a way of more securely anchoring the picture. Accordingly, he drove a six-penny nail directly into a stud in the wall and the picture was replaced. However, the next morning the picture was found again on the floor. These strange circumstances would repeat themselves many times in the days to come.

"It seemed just a little strange at the time but as I look back at it, there was something even weirder about the whole thing. That picture was really fragile—it had to be at least a hundred years old and the distance from the place where it hung to the floor was at least five feet. It should have been broken to pieces the first time it fell, but in the whole time I found it on the floor, maybe eight or ten times, it was not damaged at all. It was almost like, instead of falling off the wall, it was being taken down and carefully put on the floor."

The end to the mysterious episodes with the picture came several weeks later when Becky, out of desperation, decided to change the location of the picture. "I looked around the living room and my eyes were drawn to the opposite wall. Suddenly I saw exactly where it should be. I could almost see the picture hanging there. It was like someone was whispering in my ear *'Now that is the place for it!'* And then, when I walked over to where I thought it should go, I found a small hole in the wall, where a picture evidently been hung there years before. I shook my head and hung the picture there and it stayed there, undisturbed, for the rest of our time in the house."

As puzzling as the incidents with the picture seemed, neither Becky nor Dale had time to spend thinking about it in the busyness of moving in and establishing themselves in their new business and community. However, as the first weeks turned to months, other odd incidents would intrude into their lives.

"The first strange thing I remember was the footsteps on the stairs," Dale remembers. "There is a steep staircase that leads from the first floor where the funeral business is to the second floor where we were living. I walked up those stairs probably a dozen times a day and I knew the sound that each step made.

"Well, I remember one night I came upstairs late after a visitation and I shut the door to the stairs and went straight to the kitchen and poured myself a cup of coffee. I sat there for a few minutes, just think-ing, and was about to get up and go to bed when I heard footsteps coming up the stairs. They were clear as day and I could tell which stair was being stepped on. I thought for a minute and figured that maybe Bob Johnson, who was still working with us at that point, had come in late and needed to talk to me.

"By then, the footsteps had stopped right outside the door and I waited for someone to knock, but nothing happened. So I went to the door and opened it, but no one was there. There was no way that some-one could have gotten back down those stairs in the time it took me to get to the door and I would have heard them if they did, but the stair-way was just empty." Cautiously, Dale went downstairs and searched the area, but he found all the doors locked and the only resident to be the body in Sitting Room Two.

Dale goes on to relate that he continued to hear the footsteps peri-odically for years afterward, but at first he was reluctant to tell his wife about them. "It was enough that I had carted this poor girl to live in a funeral home, but to tell her that something weird was going on was not a prospect that I wanted to deal with until I had to."

As it turned out, Dale did not have to wait long before discussing the phantom footsteps. In fact, it was Becky who brought the subject up to him. "It was a spring night the year after we had moved in," Dale now says. "We had two visitations going on at once and I had been working solid for twelve hours. Finally about ten o'clock, the last visitor left and I stayed downstairs doing paperwork for about an hour more. Then I came upstairs, bone tired. I slipped into bed, expecting Becky to be asleep, but she wasn't. When I asked her why she was still awake she said to me, 'Well, how could I sleep with you climbing up and down those stairs all night!' "

Realizing the significance of his wife's comment, Dale asked her about what it was she had heard. She told him that during the course of the evening she had repeatedly heard footsteps climbing up the stairs to their living quarters, but the door, which was closed, was never opened. "She thought it odd that I would be coming up the stairs but not coming in," Dale says. "I reluctantly told her that I had been downstairs the entire time. Gratefully, she seemed to take it in stride." Indeed, Becky did seem to take the news that there might be another presence in the house with a certain calmness and even humor. "I think that it just sort of evolved," she says with a chuckle. "First, I fall in love with a guy who is a funeral director, then I am living in a funeral home, and the next thing I know, we have a ghost. My attitude was sort of 'what's next?' In the end it did not bother me all that much."

Now that both Dale and Becky had come to the realization that something otherworldly might be happening around them, they began taking notice of other odd happenings. "It was not all that dramatic stuff," Dale says today. "Sometimes it was just simple things that I noticed."

Dale says that he frequently developed the distinct feeling of another presence in the home, particularly when he was working on the first floor at night. "I would be in the back preparing a body for showing and I would suddenly realize that I felt like there was someone else in the room—I felt like if I turned around quick enough I would catch somebody looking over my shoulder but I knew I was alone. It was unsettling the first few times, but after a while I just sort of got used to it."

Other small incidents continued to compile themselves. Often, Dale reports that he would take a break from working during the day to get a cup of coffee from the pot in the lounge area of the funeral home. This pot was customarily kept full and hot to serve the needs of visiting family members. However, many times Dale would go to the lounge, pour himself a cup of coffee and return to his desk in the office only to find the coffee ice cold. "I would go back to the coffee pot I had poured it from thirty seconds before and find the coffee was steaming hot, but somehow my coffee had gone cold in seconds. It never seemed to happen to anyone else but me, but it happened quite often and in fact it still occasionally does," Dale reports.

Another story Dale tells also centers around the coffee pot in the family lounge. Since the pot was kept plugged in constantly during the day to keep the coffee warm for visitors, one of the last things Dale did each night after closing was to unplug it. To leave the pot plugged in would, of course, present a fire hazard. However, on several occasions, when he ventured into the room late at night, he would find the job of unplugging the coffee pot had already been done. Often this occurred when no one had been near the room all evening. To further add to the mystery, Dale says that not only was the pot unplugged, but the cord was wound around the base of the pot, eliminating any possibility that it had been accidentally unplugged.

Becky also reports several peculiar episodes occurring in the Kuzemka's living quarters on the second floor. One of the strangest occurred after living in the home for three years, when Dale installed an intercom system from the first floor office to their kitchen on the second floor. "Dale thought it would be convenient for his workers to call up to him when they needed help, so he installed this complex system. The first week we got the system in, it worked fine," Becky recalls, "but then the dumb thing just went berserk. The intercom buzzer started going off at all hours of the day and night. I had Dale call the company that installed it and they checked the whole thing out but could find nothing wrong. So, we had the whole system replaced. That worked for about a month and then it all started again."

What made the odd malfunction of the intercom even stranger was that the incoming calls seemed to originate from one location. "The system was set up so that I could look and see where the call was coming from in the building." Becky says. "I almost hate to say it, but all of the incoming calls seemed to come from the preparation room, where the bodies are embalmed and made ready for showing. Most of the time, I knew that Dale was not in that room and, believe me, nobody else there ever wants to talk."

Still the calls continued, until one night when alone in the house, Becky received several beeps in a row from the preparation room. Out of desperation, she finally unplugged the intercom from the wall and went to bed. Whoever, or whatever was trying to reach out from the first floor, however, was not so easily thwarted.

"About one o'clock that morning I woke up to hear that familiar beep. I was so sleepy it did not occur to me that the system was un-plugged till I got to the kitchen. There the intercom was, plugged back into the wall with the light showing an incoming call…from the prepa-ration room."

Becky also reports other unexplained incidents in the house, in-cluding noises coming from the third floor above the section where she and her husband were living. "The third floor, which is now used for storage, was then just a large empty room. I'm told that Alvin Johnson actually built it for parties and entertaining, which is a little strange in and of itself I guess, but when we got there it was just empty except for a few old filing cabinets and a discarded chest of drawers sitting along one wall."

Still, several times during their years in the home, Dale and Becky Kuzemka were disturbed to hear sounds emanating from the empty room above their heads. "The first thing I remember," Dale says, "was waking up one night and hearing the sound of something heavy being dragged across the floor. It sounded like someone moving a huge piece of furniture. I thought to myself, 'Now what the hell is *this*?' So, after listening to the racket for a few minutes I got up the courage to go up there. Since the lights were disconnected to that floor, I had to use a flashlight and I will admit that I was a little spooked. But when I got up there, there was absolutely nothing out of the ordinary. The few things that were in that room were undisturbed and the dust on the floor showed that nothing had been touched or moved in quite some time."

Becky also recalls hearing voices coming to her ear from the third floor. She describes the instance as hearing several voices, as though in pleasant conversation, coming down from the third floor expanse. "It was not distinct—I couldn't make out any exact words but it sounded very much like several people talking up there. I do remember at least once hearing a woman's laugh. It was eerie, I can tell you. I knew the door was locked and the third floor was empty at the time."

Still, despite the growing evidence of something "otherworldly" sharing their abode, the Kuzemkas were reluctant to talk about their experiences. "Not many people want to send their loved ones to a haunted funeral home," Dale says with a good-natured grin. "That is one of the reasons I do not want my name or the name of my funeral home printed in this book. At first, we did not tell anyone that we were noticing anything funny, until two years after we bought the place, when Bob Johnson was finally retiring.

"The summer before he finally left the business," he continues, "Bob and I were sitting in the office one afternoon talking business. He said that he was looking forward to moving to Florida, but he still hated to leave the funeral home he and his dad had invested so much of their lives building. I remember he smiled and said, 'But I know I am leaving the business in good hands. I am leaving you to take care of this business—but dad will help you look after it too.' I was startled when he said that and shot him a look that must have given away more than I intended. Bob smiled and said 'Come on, you must have been around here long enough by now to know that dad still comes back occasionally. I have known it since right after he died. Don't be scared—he wouldn't hurt anybody. I think he just loves the place so much he can't quite let go.' "

Perhaps the elder Mr. Johnson did indeed retain an interest in the funeral home he had established and if this is the case, he might well have been upset when the business was finally completely handed over to someone outside the family. This was evidenced by the fact that in the weeks after Bob Johnson's departure to Florida, the occurrences seemed to pick up with a vengeance.

"This was just about the time the intercom went nuts," Dale recalls. "Right after Bob left us for the last time, all kinds of things went on. I came into the casket room one morning to help a family pick out a casket and found that all of the lids on the coffins had been closed. That was strange because we always had a habit of leaving them open so that folks could view the interiors. Then, that same day, I came into my office to find that a file folder I had left on my desk had been opened and the papers scattered all over the room. I knew that I was the only one in the office that day and there was no way a breeze could have scattered them like that. I even found one paper lying on one of the blades of the ceiling fan in the room."

It was about that time that Becky, too began to notice an increase in supernatural activity. "I remember one night when I suddenly woke up for no reason. I had been dead asleep and then I suddenly was awake and sat bolt upright in the bed," she says. "I tried to listen to see if there was some noise that had awakened me, but it was all quiet. So, after checking the doors, I went to the bathroom and then went back to bed. As I left the bathroom heading back toward the bedroom, I distinctly felt someone reach out and touch my right shoulder. It was a hand—I know it was—and I turned and kind of yelled but no one was there. In a second, Dale came steaming out of the bedroom like an avenging angel, thinking that someone had broken in, but I had to tell him to go back to bed—our ghost was at it again. Looking back at it, I was not so much scared at that moment as I was just startled."

Several months after Dale Kuzemka took over the running of the business completely, the phenomena seemed to slacken a bit. "I have thought before that old Alvin just needed to know we were going to take care of the place and when he figured out we were OK he took it a little easier on us," Dale remarks.

Still, in the suceeding years, the odd incidents have continued to occur. The notion that Alvin Johnson was indeed returning to his former residence was augmented a few years after Dale took over the business, when he and Becky were blessed with a baby daughter. "For growing up in a funeral home, our daughter's early growing up years were pretty normal," Becky says. "Linda got used to the fact of where we lived pretty quickly. As a young girl, she would go down to the office and play in the casket room when she got bored. Some people would think that is morbid, but we did not think much about it. It was pretty normal for our family."

However, one incident that occurred with the young girl might not be considered quite so normal. "When Linda was about three or four, she, like many children, began to play with imaginary playmates," Becky fondly recalls. "There for a while, we got regular visits from Mighty Mouse or Superman. I think that Cinderella even visited on occasion."

As time wore on, Dale and Becky began to notice their daughter begin to repeatedly speak about one imaginary friend more and more frequently. "She just called him 'the man' and she said he was her best friend," Becky now says. "We did not think much about it until one day I was walking by her room and heard her talking, apparently to no one. I stopped to listen and realized she was talking to one of her imaginary friends. She would ask a question and then pause as though she was listening to a reply. It sounded so real, it really struck me, so that night as I was tucking her into bed, after we said our prayers, I asked her who she had been talking to."

With a broad smile the child told her mother that she had been talking to her friend, "the man." When Becky pressed her for a description of her friend, she said that he was like Superman—he could fly, or at least float off the ground, and could even walk through walls. More amused than concerned, Becky asked her daughter what she and the man talked about. "All kinds of things," came the reply. "The man said that he watches me sometimes and likes my games. He tells me about our house—he knows how it was a long time ago." It was this last comment that, Becky reports, sent a chill down her spine. Still reasoning that her daughter might well be imagining her new friend and that, at the very least, if it was a ghost, he was an apparently benevolent one, she let the matter drop.

However, the subject of their daughter's invisible friend would become the topic of conversation again several months later, when Linda and her father were in the downstairs office one rainy afternoon. "I remember that day quite well," Dale says, "because business was slow and since it was raining, Linda was bored and so she came downstairs to keep me company. I was using the slow time to go though some old papers in the filing cabinet and we were dragging out the files together and looking at them. When I got to a file of old newspaper clippings, I happened to flip open the file to an old story on the funeral home and at the bottom of the page was a picture of Alvin Johnson standing in front of the house."

"When Linda saw that, she sucked in her breath and pointed to the picture and excitedly yelled 'My friend, Daddy! My friend! That is the man!' I told her it was just an old picture but she assured me that this was the nice man who came and talked to her in her room sometimes. She was so excited that she had to take the clipping upstairs to show her mother. Needless to say, Becky and I had a long talk about the picture that night after Linda was in bed."

To their credit, the Kuzemka's seem to have adapted well to living and working around what they refer to as "our resident spook." While they are still very reticent to speak of the ghost to their friends or business acquaintances, within the family they have learned to live with what they consider to be the ghost of the former owner.

"He really is a nice enough spook," Dale reflects with some irony. "At his worst, he is just mischievous and at his best, he can be helpful. The worst thing he ever did to me was to douse a cigar I was smoking on the back patio.

"That happened about five years ago and coincidently happened when an old friend of Mr. Johnson's had come over for the visit. He had known the family for many years and we had become good friends since I moved to town. He had just come back from Canada and he knew I loved cigars, so he had brought us each back a couple of good Cuban cigars."

"He came to visit me on a Saturday afternoon," Dale continues, "and since it was my day off he and I went to the back patio for a Coke and so that we could try out the cigars. After we had been there a while, I mentioned some remodeling that we had done to the second floor and offered to show him what was being done. So we left our cigars in ashtray on the table and went upstairs. When we got back to the porch a few minutes later, we found that the cigars were still in the ashtray but someone had poured my glass of pop all over them. It ruined a couple of perfectly good cigars.

"When I picked up my cigar, my friend looked at me kind of funny and said 'Does your wife or daughter not appreciate your smoking?' I told him that my wife and daughter were in town shopping and that we were the only ones around. I was afraid he might be put off with this bit of news, but instead he just smiled and said, 'Then maybe it is old Alvin saying hello. He always hated smoking anyway and never allowed anyone to smoke in the house.' I stared down at that drowned cigar and thought that I could put up with a ghost in the house but he darn well better learn to put up with a cigar now and again."

If the spirit of the Johnson funeral home has at times shown a mischievous bent, it should also be noted that on other occasions, it has also manifested a more benevolent and even helpful disposition as well. As noted earlier, the spirit has been credited with unplugging appliances that have been left unattended and even turning off lights that have inadvertently been left on at night. Another dramatic instance of such accommodating behavior occurred in 1989.

"I remember it well," Dale Kuzemka says. "In fact, this is one thing I cannot forget." On that particular day, Dale says his energies were being taxed to their breaking point. Already shorthanded because one of his workers had recently undergone surgery and another was called out of town unexpectedly on family business, Dale was faced with the prospect of setting up his viewing rooms for two large funerals that would take place just a few hours apart.

"I remember I was running around like crazy," Dale says. "On top of everything else, we had just had all the carpets in the place cleaned the day before and I had to reset 150 chairs in the viewing rooms in less than two hours. I had asked a friend to help me move the chairs into the rooms, where we just sort of stacked them in bunches till I could get around to replacing them where they went. After about an hour of just moving the chairs into their respective rooms, my wife called us upstairs for a bite of lunch. We were upstairs no more than fifteen minutes when I told them that I had to get back to work."

"I went back down the stairs and went into Room One and proceeded to set about arranging the chairs. It was hot work and I was really tired about forty-five minutes later when I was done." Checking his watch and realizing that he had little more than an hour before family and guests would begin arriving, Dale then hastily moved across the hall to the second room to begin the task anew.

"I unlocked the door to Room Two," Dale remembers, "and I could not believe my eyes. The chairs were set up in perfect rows, just the way I would have put them. My first thought is that my wife and friend had come down to help out but I had not heard them. Then I remembered that the door had been locked and I was the only person in the building with a key. Still, just to make sure, I went upstairs and asked them if they had replaced the chairs in Room Two. They were sitting drinking coffee and both looked at me like I was crazy. They swore up and down that they had not left the kitchen on the second floor. What make it doubly strange is that the two rooms are just a few feet from one another and I sure should have heard anyone moving heavy chairs in that room. I guess it is still a mystery but all the same, I am grateful to whoever had replaced those chairs."

As dramatic as this incident was, it is not the only time the ghost of the Johnson Funeral home has shown such a helpful propensity. Indeed, another such occasion may be the only known instance of the spirit showing itself to someone who did not work in the funeral home.

"It was another time when I was super busy," Dale says. "It was a night in October of 1997 and we had a visitation going on. Two of my workers had gone out to pick up a body from the local hospital. I was standing talking with the family in the visitation room when one of my guys came in and told me they had arrived with the body and would need my help in unloading it from the hearse. I excused myself and was leaving the room when a friend of the family stopped me—a middle-aged woman from out of town. She told me that she loved the old house and asked me about its history. Being somewhat rushed at that moment, I told her that I had to attend to some business, but would be happy to talk to her when I returned in a few minutes.

"Then I went into the back to help my workers. It was probably half an hour later when I came back to the viewing room and saw the same lady standing in the corner talking with the family. I went over to her to apologize for not speaking to her earlier and began to tell her about the story of the house. I had only gotten out a few sentences when she interrupted me by saying, 'You don't have to worry, one of your workers already has told me all about the house.' I was puzzled because the workers had been with me in the back, but I asked her as casually as I could which worker she had spoken to. She told me it was the elderly man who had come down the stairs form the second floor. She said he seemed quite knowledgable about the house and its history and she had enjoyed their chat.

"Now," Dale Kuzemka says today, the smoke from one of his beloved cigars curling past a wry smile, "after hearing the rest of my story, do I have to mention that we had no worker fitting that description on duty that night?"

Indeed he does not. In fact, after reviewing the whole of his story, perhaps such an occurrence might seem queerly in tune with the atmosphere of the place.

In 1998, Dale and his family, expecting their second child, purchased a more spacious home in town and moved from their living quarters at Johnson Funeral Home. Both Dale and his wife Becky flatly deny, however, that their resident ghost had anything to do with their decision to move. "If anything, I had come to accept our resident spook," Becky muses. "I mean, after all, it was his house first and who were we to wish him gone?"

Since that time, Dale has continued to encounter the occasional odd phenomena while at work, but he now has a more peaceful existence at home. "We still get the occasional bump in the night when I work late," Dale reports, "and just last month, one of my new workers came to me to ask if I had been the one walking up and down the stairs the evening before. But, overall, I guess that I notice the spook a little less than I did before. Still, the whole place still feels like it belongs to him."

Perhaps it does. Perhaps, in the final analysis, the stately funeral home sitting so serenely on a tree-lined street in this small Indiana town will always belong to the spirit of its founder. Maybe this place that serves the departed and their families with dignity and compassion will always contain the spirit of at least one who has never entirely departed this life and will remain a fixture in this beautiful home forever.

6
WHEN DARKNESS COMES TO CENTRAL STATE
Indianapolis, Indiana[6]

"Be careful not to conjure up more phantoms than you can put down."
—*Old Welsh Proverb*

Each night darkness comes to the grounds of the former Central State Hospital once again. Nearby, in the thriving heart of this metropolitan city, night is merely an illusion, broken by the harsh incandescence of street lamps or stained the gaudy colors of neon lights. But across this sprawling landscape, the night is something more...something that seems to take on a life of its own. Here the darkness is palpable. It creeps over the grounds, seeping through the cracks of boarded-up doorways and stealing down dusty halls now long abandoned.

Here the clouds passing over the pale face of the moon cast strange, misshapen shadows on the lawn. Windows of empty buildings stare unseeing into the gloom and the distant murmur of traffic is quickly lost to the pervading, ominous silence that blankets the grounds.

Here the night has a pulse and a breath that brings with it a cool dampness as from the crypt. This breath whispers through the leaves of the tall oak trees that dot the landscape, sighing and gently moaning along the wrought iron fence that separates the grounds from the city that surrounds it. It is this breath that wraps itself around the mute structures in an unearthly caress.

Here there are things not fully alive and yet not quite dead. Troubled voices murmur from the past and, perhaps, as some would suggest, even more...spirits hungering for a freedom and healing they never found in life.

When all is said and done, perhaps the tales told of the place may be simply attributed to the night. Possibly these stories that have been born of the night may take their only reality from it. However, according to the belief of some, there may be more to them than just moon shadow and wind. Perhaps the night brings with it something mysterious to this place, strange echoes of a sometimes tragic past—voices at once pitiful and plaintive, even more so in death than they once were in life.

The story of Central State Hospital is one of hope and despair, promise and anguish, extraordinary care and inhuman cruelty. It is a story of souls mended and lives extinguished. It is the story of an institution once venerated for its pioneering efforts in the treatment of mental illness, and yet rumors of horrific abuse persist that, in part, caused the hospital's ultimate demise.

The story begins in 1827, when the Indiana Legislature authorized the establishment of a "hospital for the insane." Plans for this venture were formulated, but due to delays (primarily with state funding) it was not until 1848 that the "Indiana Hospital for the Insane" opened its doors in the young city of Indianapolis. At the time of its inauguration, the institution consisted of one brick building located on one hundred wooded acres. However, demands placed on the hospital and staff soon dictated the expansion of the facility, and over the next half-century many more buildings quickly arose within the fenced enclosure.

Eventually, a huge gothic building called "Seven Steeples" was built for housing women patients, as well as a similar dormitory for men. A chapel, a "sick hospital" (for the treatment of patients suffering from physical as well as psychiatric conditions), and a host of other buildings soon sprang up among the tall oaks that dot the campus.

The buildings were badly needed, for the steady inflow of patients greatly increased with the passing years. While today, inpatient psychiatric hospitals are generally reserved for patients with severe emotional or psychological stress, in the nineteenth century, the term "insane" had a broad and varied definition. Those coming through the doors of Central State Hospital (as it was shortly renamed) suffered from a variety of emotional and mental illnesses. The conditions treated at the hospital spanned the spectrum from clinical depression to schizophrenia. Sadly, many warehoused at the institution were sent there because they were termed "simple," a colloquial term for mentally handicapped.

Inevitably, Central State was also known to count among its patients those diagnosed as "criminally insane." These patients, judged too prone to violence to be housed in less secure institutions, were held under tight security, and at times in the early history of the institution, were kept in a state of near-perpetual restraint. Though no firm confirmation may be ascertained, it is said that workers in the 1950s, while renovating some of the over five miles of tunnels that connected the buildings, discovered dark rooms in the recesses of the tunnels that still bore chains and manacles on their walls.

Other examples of the sometimes barbaric methods employed in retraining patients in the early days of Central State are more easily confirmed. As recorded in the official Indiana archives, on the surface, Central State Hospital seemed to be a fairly pleasant place. A closer look, however, revealed some unsavory realities. For decades in the late 1800s, the hospital confined its "worst inmates," those who screamed incessantly, or who were hostile to staff, to the basement or "dungeons" of the hospital.

Dr. Everts, superintendent of Central State in 1870, vividly reported his findings regarding the conditions there in a letter to the Governor of Indiana:

> Basement dungeons are dark, humid and foul, unfit for life of any kind, filled with maniacs who raved and howled like tortured beasts, for want of light and air and food and ordinary human associations and habiliments.

In his report to the Governor, Dr. Everts goes on to state that even the "normal" wards were "without adequate provision for light, heat and ventilation." Patients, according to his report, were forced to sleep on straw mattresses amid buildings with rotting floors and leaking roofs.

Despite Dr. Everts' pleas for funding to improve the conditions at Central State, his cries went unheard by state legislators. In 1872, Dr. Everts, frustrated in his efforts to improve the situation there, resigned in protest.

However, it should not be assumed that the entire history of Central State Hospital is one of inhumane treatment of the mentally ill. Eventually, a special committee was convened by the state legislature to investigate conditions there. Their report resulted in sweeping changes in the facility and treatment methods. By 1890, in part due to rising public awareness of abuses at the hosptial, conditions began to improve there. Use of restraints was greatly curtailed, and more attention was paid to treating rather than warehousing patients. Social activities were regularly scheduled for staff and patients, and vocational rehabilitation was introduced. It was also at this time that more scientific methods of researching the causes of mental illness were brought to the institution.

Under the superintendence of Dr. Edenharter, a new "pathology laboratory" was constructed on the edge of the hospital campus. Here hundreds of autopsies were performed on deceased patients and the results shared in lectures to medical students who regularly met there. In time, a brick annex, called the "dead house," was attached to the building to store bodies awaiting autopsy. It was hoped that by examining the physiology of the mentally ill, some physical cause for their condition could be ascertained and new cures for mental illness could be found. It seemed that a new era had arrived for mental health and in particular, for Central State Hospital.

However, despite the best efforts of superintendents through the latter part of the nineteenth century, the plight of Central State remained a mixed bag. During the twentieth century, the hospital attracted many physicians of national and international renown, and patient treatment overall continued to improve. It should be noted that many of those who worked tirelessly at Central State for many years did so with a care and selfless dedication that was a credit to their lives and profession. As a result of their efforts, many of those who passed through the halls of Central State were treated with respect and dignity. There are many people in living in Indiana today who have benefited through the time they spent at this institution.

Still, it must be noted that through the years, persistent allegations of patient neglect and abuse continued to dog the institution. Reports periodically filtered out to the press regarding the callous use of retstraints, beatings, and other abuses. Indianapolis newspapers quickly picked up on lurid and sensational tales of patient mistreatment and neglect. Overcrowded conditions, a perpetual lack of funding, and sometimes poor training of staff added to a gathering cloud over the hospital.

In the late 1970s, most of the hospital's ornate Victorian-era build-ings were declared unsound and demolished to be replaced with insti-tutional brick dormitories. However, despite the long awaited improve-ments to the physical structure of the hospital, the fate of Central State seemed cast. According to the Indiana State Archives:

> These modern buildings and the medical staff therein continued to serve the state's mentally ill, until allegations of patient abuse and funding troubles sparked an effort to forge new alternatives to institutionalization which, in turn led to the Hospital's closure.

Indeed, in 1994, riding a national trend away from large institu-tional settings, the state of Indiana closed Central State Hospital. Thus ended 146 years of service at the institution. Upon closure, the facility reverted to the control of the state which, with the help of the State Archives, chose to preserve at least some of the buildings. The old pathology building was converted for use as the Indiana Medical His-tory Museum, while the rest of the facility is maintained under the direction of the State Board of Health and guarded by the Capital Police.

In retrospect, the closure was bittersweet. While no doubt the na-tional movement in the mental health field away from warehousing patients in large institutions was good for some individuals, for others this move was tragic. The wholesale deinstitutionalization of such a large number of patients left many without adequate care or shelter. Some were left to wander the streets with sometimes-dreadful consequences.

Moreover, the closure of Central State Hospital sadly ended nearly a century and a half of history—some of it meritorious and some appalling. In the end the history of Central State, like that of many mental institutions, is a mix of pride and shame, acclaim and dishonor. For the many who served so hard and long in the care of the mentally ill, Central State will always have a place of reverence and honor. For those patients who may have lived and died in horrific circumstances there, it will forever be a place of horror.

And, according to some, the horror may not yet be over. For, it is said, that within the confines of the wrought iron fence that surrounds the Central State campus, at least some of the dead remain still. Amid the darkness that descends again each night, plaintive, poignant phantoms are said to still linger, searching for the release of suffering they never found in life. According to some, it is their cries which are heard in the deepening shadows each evening. It is their chilling presence that comes with the dark, transforming these beautiful grounds into a place that is truly of the night.

One of those who claim to have heard their voices is Louis Jarecki*, who has worked at Central State for over twenty-two years. In his time at the hospital, he has filled a variety of positions that have bought him into all areas of the hospital.

"When I first came here, " says Mr. Jarecki, his gravelly voice belying a gentle twinkle in his eye, "I worked as security. It was our job to make sure the patients stayed put, and that was not always easy. Occasionally, we had to wrestle with some of the more violent patients in order to keep them from hurting themselves. Then, after a while, I went to work in the boiler room maintaining the steam pipes in the buildings. When the main boiler room was shut down, I went to work in the electrical shop."

Since the hospital shut down, Mr. Jarecki has continued to work in a variety of functions there, from general maintenance to night security. As such, he has been privy to some unsettling and seemingly inexplicable occurrences there.

"What you have to understand is that I hear them all the time", Mr. Jarecki says, his eyes suddenly turning serious. "Anybody could. You have to be perceptive, but you can definitely hear them." His grave demeanor is understandable, for the "them" to which Jarecki is referring are the sounds that he has heard while making his nightly rounds of the hospital. "You hear them on the grounds," he continues. "It is crying—sometimes screaming, like you used to hear when the patients were still here. While I worked here, we had patients who would scream constantly and who suffered. We even had one patient who hung himself. Sometimes at night you can still hear them scream and moan."

Although Mr. Jarecki says that he had heard these noises all throughout the hospital campus, one area in particular has drawn his attention more than once. It is an area that he says has a morbid past. According to Jarecki, at one time a patient was stoned to death by another patient in a grove of trees that shade one side of the grounds. "I remember that the patient who did it was immediately shipped to Logansport Hospital afterward," he now says. "But when you walk by that grove of trees at night you can still hear the screaming and moaning coming from it."

As disturbing as these sounds are, they have not been Louis Jarecki's only contact with the inexplicable at Central State. "I have also seen things," he flatly states. "At night, when I have been working the guard shack, I have seen what look like patients run by and into the street. They just look like a blur. You see, those gates used to be there to help keep some of the patients in the hospital, and every so often, one of them would try to get out by running past the gates. We guards would have to go after them. Several times since the patients have been moved out, I have still seen these figures."

Some might well attribute such sightings as a trick of light as seen through the tired eyes of a night watchman. Louis Jarecki, however, believes they are the spiritual remnants of patients who are still seeking their freedom, even after their mortal lives have ended.

Were Jarecki the only member of the Central Hospital staff to report such occurrences, his information might be viewed with skepticism if not outright disbelief. However, many other current and former workers at the institution have their own tales to tell. Another present employee at the hospital, Ben Gray*, speaks of a great many such experiences. Like Mr. Jarecki, through his job Gray has often been called to work at Central State at night, performing routine maintenance. At such times, he too reports having heard strange and eerie sounds coming to his ear through the cool night air.

"Over in the old power house, we used to have to go down and pull ashes twice during our shift at night," Mr. Gray says. "It was dark and eerie down there, even during the day, I can tell you. At nighttime it seemed a lot worse, somehow. We would go down there and pull ashes while the boiler operator stayed upstairs at his post. That's when it would happen. I swear we used to hear what sounded like a woman screaming and moaning in the corner. We would look around and search the place, but there wasn't anyone down there but us."

At other times, things in the boiler room got even stranger. "I used to sit there, while we took a break from shoveling the ashes and I would swear that I could see shadows or people moving from column to column. There are several big columns in the room and I would catch their movement between them. It got me so scared that I looked all over the place and could find nothing. I absolutely knew that I saw something down there out of the corner of my eye."

As strange as these experiences were for Gray, they pale in comparison with an incident a coworker reported to him one night at the same maintenance building. "I had a coworker, Ron, who got really spooked" he now recalls. "He was down there in the one of the pump rooms taking a nap late one night. I was taking a break with the other guys on the main floor when he came up white as a sheet—he was just scared to death. I took one look at him and said 'What's the matter with you?' "

In a shaky voice, the coworker explained that he had been awakened from his illicit sleep in the basement with the strong sensation of being strangled.

"He said to me, 'Someone was choking me down there,' " Mr. Gray reports. "Then he went on to say, 'I could feel the hands around my neck but when I broke loose and went and turned on the light there was nobody down there.' I told him he was nuts—that he had just had a bad dream. But he looked me square in the eye and said 'Oh yeah, what about this?' Then he pulled down the neck of his shirt and sure enough, there were deep red marks on his throat, just like somebody had put their hands there and pressed."

Ben Gray concludes his story by noting that from that point on, his fellow employee steadfastly refused to enter the pump rooms of the building. "One time we were told to go down there and fix the pump," Gray recalls, "and he refused. He said, 'I will quit if I have to go down there.' So I had to go get someone else to help me fix the pump."

Mr. Gray also reports odd instances of electrical devices apparently turning themselves on without the aid of any human agent. "In the basement of the old power house," he explains, "we had a conveyer belt that used to be used to carry coal to the boiler. There was a switch for it on the far wall and I remember you had to press it hard to turn it on.

"Well, one night I was in that room with the boiler operator and we were the only ones in the building," he continues. "We were sitting at a table just talking, when suddenly we heard the click of the switch on the far side of the room and the belt turned on. We were shocked but we went over and turned it off again and then we searched that whole area, but we were the only ones there.

"Later," Gray remembers with a wry smile, "we were walking out of the building and as we walked to the door, we heard a hum coming from the basement we had just come from. We listened for a minute and realized that it sounded like that conveyer belt had turned itself on again. I asked the other man with me if he wanted to go down and see what was going on, but he said 'There is no way in hell I'm going back down there!' I agreed, so we locked up the building and left."

Voices and the hum of a conveyor belt that should not be on are not the only things Gray has apparently heard while in the precincts of Central State Hospital. He claims other sounds resound through the administration building late at night. "A lot of times, I am in the administration building at night all by myself," he says. "Many times I have heard what sound like footsteps going up and down the halls. At first I thought they were just the sounds of animals and then I realized that they were animals wearing high heels."

One particular instance remains clear in his memory. "I was in the main office in the administration building, sitting back in a chair with my eyes closed," he recalls, "when I heard the clear sound of footsteps crossing the tile floor of the main lobby. They walked across the lobby and came straight toward to the big sliding window at the front of the office. I thought maybe someone had come into the building unexpectedly so I got up quick and went to the window, but there was no one there.

"However, as I stood there looking into the empty lobby," he adds, "I could hear the footsteps walking away from the window into the building. I could trace where the person should have been from the sound of the steps but no one was there at all. I know it all sounds crazy, but let me tell you, there are some pretty strange things that go on here at night."

Ben Gray is not alone in this supposition. While it must be said that many who work and have worked around the facility claim no such experiences with the supernatural, in talking with many others, a surprising number of strange stories quickly come to light.

Sandra Torreson* was a psychiatric nurse at Central State for six years, from 1986 until its closure in 1994. While she readily states that she is an "agnostic with regard to things ghostly," many of the stories she heard while working at the hospital and at least one or two of her own experiences have given her reason to wonder.

"No one talked about the stories all that much," Ms. Torreson says. "I don't think the administration was all that wild about its staff talking about ghosts, but still, after I had been there a while, a couple of the older nurses mentioned what they had seen and heard. It was pretty weird stuff."

One story in particular has haunted her ever since. "I remember when I heard the story," she recalls. "It was a year after I started working at the hospital when a couple of girls and I went out for coffee after work."

Over coffee, the nurses began to talk about their place of employment and one stated that she refused to enter the "catacombs" (as the long tunnels that connected the building were called) after dark. Then she cryptically added, "Especially since Agnes told me about talking to her friend down there."

Intrigued, Ms. Torreson asked her coworker about the story of Agnes and the woman quickly warmed to her tale. As she recalls the story, it seems that several years before, a male patient named Alvin was suddenly found to be missing from the institution. While Alvin was on a "nonsecure" ward and not considered dangerous to himself or others, still an alarm was posted. All the buildings at Central State were searched from top to bottom, with no result. Local police were notified and all staff were told to be on the lookout for the missing patient.

According to Ms. Torreson, the nurse who told the story said that as time passed and no sign of Alvin had been found, it was assumed that he had somehow wandered off into the streets of Indianapolis and that he would never be seen again. This might well have remained the popular opinion, except for the odd behavior of a female patient some months later.

"My friend told me that one of the women on her ward, a lady named Agnes, suddenly began wandering off," she now relates. "She would just disappear from the ward and they would have to search for her. Inevitably, she would be found on the steps that led down in the catacombs, just sitting by herself. It got to be so regular that when she disappeared, instead of calling security they would just send one of the nurses down there to bring her back up."

Ms. Torreson goes on to say that her coworker told of one night when Agnes, true to form, disappeared from the ward and she was told to go down and persuade her to return to her room. The nurse in question went and found the patient in her customary place on the stairs leading down to the tunnels.

"My friend said that as they were walking back to the ward, just out of curiosity, she asked Agnes why she liked to go down there and Agnes told her 'I go down there to talk with my friend.' She said she was about to dismiss the remark as merely the fantasy of a delusional patient until the woman said, 'His name is Alvin and he says he lives in the tunnel.'"

The remark caught the attention of the nurse, who realized the significance of the name Agnes had just mentioned. Returning to her ward, the nurse immediately called the security office and asked if the missing patient, Alvin, had yet been found. When the chief told her he had not, she suggested that the tunnel beneath her building be searched and related the story told to her by the patient. It was her thought that somehow the patient Alvin might not have escaped at all, but had merely wandered into the tunnels and had somehow managed to survive there.

That afternoon, members of the security staff combed the tunnel beneath the women's ward, once more to no avail. They were about to give up when one officer noticed the grate leading to a small crawl space ajar. Carefully he removed the grate and, using his flashlight, entered the small area.

There he found the still body that used to be Alvin. It was all too clear that the man had been dead for several months; thus resolving the mystery of Alvin's disappearance. However this led to an even more odd question: how could a patient who had no contact with Alvin in life claim to visit with him regularly in the weeks after his death? It is a question that today still haunts some familiar with the story.

"When my friend got done telling her story, there was dead silence at the table," Ms. Torreson says. "You could have heard a pin drop. But then several of the other woman at the table exploded with stories of their own."

According to Ms. Torreson, another nurse, who had been at Central State for many years, told of another strange experience. The nurse claimed that while exploring the tunnels many years before, she had discovered an adjacent room with a dirt floor and manacles attached to the walls. Repulsed by the sight, she quickly left the room and continued with her explorations, yet several months later, while walking past that particular room, she was terrified to hear the sound of moaning coming from within. Mrs. Torreson continues that the nurse who related the story told of how she steeled her nerve and opened the door to the room, only to find it dark and utterly empty.

Understandably, the stunned nurse slammed the door and fled the tunnel. Ms. Torreson remembers that the nurse who told the tale concluded it by relating that, months afterward, when she finally confided the incident to her supervisor, she was told, "Oh, never mind that. We all know about that room and we all stay away from it. A lot of us have heard those things."

Interestingly, Ms. Torreson herself notes that the only time she personally encountered anything strange while at Central State was in January 1994, shortly before the hospital closed. "At the time, we were already starting to transfer patients to other hospitals," Ms. Torreson recalls, "and there was a lot of commotion on the ward. I was working the late shift and I spent most of my time trying to get the patients to calm down and go to sleep. Finally, about 3 A.M., things finally got quiet and I sat down for a minute to catch my breath."

As Ms. Torreson tells the story, her well-deserved break that night was disturbed several minutes later by the sound of a woman's sobs floating to her ear from the direction of a dark hallway. With a sigh of resignation, Ms. Torreson rose from her chair and wandered down the hall, ready to calm whatever patient had become distraught in the night. However, as she neared the source of the sound, she quickly realized that they were coming from a patient room that was supposed to be empty, its occupants having already been transferred to another institution.

"I thought to myself, 'Now, who has gotten into this empty room?' " Ms. Torreson says. "I was not too happy that someone had gotten out of their bed in the night and gone into another room. At the door I paused for a moment and listened to the sobbing coming from inside. There was something about it that made all the hair on my arms stand up. It was heartbreaking—like someone inside was in incredible pain or distress. But when I opened the door, the crying suddenly just stopped and there was no one there. The room was empty—even the beds were gone. I stood there and in that moment I was scared to death."

As strange as the event was, it was not the last of Ms. Torreson's encounters with the unexplained that night. She goes on to say that, shocked and disturbed by her experience in the apparently empty room, she returned to her desk and quickly poured herself a cup of coffee to calm her shaken nerves.

"As I sat there, I tried to make sense of what had happened. I tried to tell myself that maybe it was my imagination, or the wind, or *anything* but I knew what I had heard," she recalls. "Then, while I was thinking about it all, I kind of subconsciously looked down to the end of the hall where the room was and I saw this hazy kind of shadow floating in front of the room. I turned my head and stared in that direction and at that moment, it zipped down the hall and disappeared into the wall at the end of the hallway. It took just a moment and it was gone but I know I saw something."

By now shaken, Ms. Torreson decided to sit out the rest of her shift at her desk and hope that she was not called to tend to a patient. Gratefully, she now reports, she was not.

Although the nurse's sighting of a hazy shadow in the hallway may sound bizarre, it is interesting to note that it correlates with the experience of a Capital Police officer in 1997. As a part of the Capital Police force (an extension of the Indiana State Police entrusted the task of guarding state-owned buildings in and around Indianapolis), it was his occasion to respond to a call at Central State Hospital. The call stated that a workman had seen movement in an upstairs window in the now abandoned women's dormitory.

The officer later told the story to a fellow police officer, and what follows is a secondhand account of that experience.

The policeman drove to Central State that night and entered the building, his flashlight the only illumination because there was no electricity running to the building. He carefully and silently made his way to the second floor where the movement had been sighted and began the task of searching every room for any sign of an intruder. He was almost to the end of the hallway when, exiting a room, he was suddenly startled by the sound of a woman's high-pitched cry. As he later reported to his friend:

> I spun around and saw what looked like a woman in a robe run past me down the hallway. She was kind of hazy but I could see her in the flashlight beam. Before I could draw my gun or even call for her to stop, she ran right into a wall at the end of the hallway and disappeared through it.

Shaken by the sight, this veteran officer exited the building and returned to his station, vowing to never again visit Central State if it could be avoided.

Nor is this officer alone in his experiences. It is said that recently, two Capital Police officers were dispatched to Central State on another late night call regarding movement seen in one of the buildings there. As they walked through the hallways, with their flashlights in hand, suddenly both their lights extinguished themselves simultaneously.

As a fellow officer comments, "Those flashlights are the hundred-dollar cop flashlights. They are built so that you can immerse them in water, run them over with a truck, and drop them over a cliff and they will still work. That one would go out is strange, but when both went out at the same time...I guess those officers nearly ran over each other getting out of there." Their haste, of course, can be understood. Perhaps it is best not to tarry too long in a place where the night holds sway in deep and mysterious ways.

It should be carefully noted that the exact historical veracity of the ghostly tales told of Central State cannot be verified. The Indiana Board of Health, which currently owns the Central State campus, categorically denies that there are any ghostly activities there and many who work at the site will agree.

Perhaps, after all, these tales are nothing more than stories born of the darkness and chill that seems to hold these grounds in their grip each night. Perhaps, after all, there is nothing more here in this once vaunted institution than moonlight and shadow.

But if one asks some current and past employees of Central State, they will tell you differently. They will tell you that when the darkness comes each night to this place, it carries something with it— something not fully alive and yet not quite dead, troubled voices from the past and, perhaps, as some would suggest, even more. Perhaps they are spirits pleading for a freedom and healing they never found in life. According to the tales told, they are the spirits of the night at Central State Hospital.

7

THE GENTLE SPIRIT OF KAHLER SCHOOL

Dyer, Indiana[7]

"We prefer to call them 'Spiritual Emanations!'"
*—Mrs. Halcyon Maxwell, **The Ghost and Mr. Chicken***

Schools are places whose very nature is tied inexorably to life. Take a walk down the hall of any elementary, middle or high school during the class day and one is instantly surrounded by the sounds of activity. The hallways resound with the frantic bustle of young people scurrying to and from class, seeking to avoid the dreaded bell that will call them tardy. The sounds of a choir painstakingly inching their way up and down the musical scale float from the chorus room, and from the gymnasium comes the rhythmic cadence of a basketball being dribbled down court. Standing in such a setting, with the reverberation of vitality and energy teeming around you, it is easy to imagine no more lively a place on earth than within the walls of our beloved schools.

It is this link with life that makes even more macabre the tales of haunted schools that dot our state. While by no means as common as the "garden variety" ghost that seems content to while away its after-life haunting a house or graveyard, it must be noted that ghostly tales linked to schools do exist in Indiana. As has been documented in an earlier work, no less than three schools in Indianapolis are said to host resident phantoms, and at least one abandoned schoolhouse in Brown

County is said to still retain the spiritual residue of students who have definitely "stayed after class." Were it not for the reluctance of school administrators to admit to a connection to such stories, many more tales of haunted schools might well come to light.

However, in the northwest corner of Indiana, there stands one school that seems to take a certain pride in the ghostly tales associated with it. Kahler Middle School sits just off of U.S.-30 in the town of Dyer, a few short blocks from the Illinois line. It is apropos that the school sits behind a large Catholic church, and in particular a small cemetery which one must pass in order to get to the front doors of the school.

Kahler Middle School looks very much the model of what a modern, efficient educational institution can be. Clean, cheerful and thoroughly up-to-date inside and out, Kahler is the educational home to over 980 students and teachers. This number, it should be assumed, represents the *living* occupants of the school. Yet if one talks to some who have had experiences in and around the school, one might well wonder if the number of souls counted there should be raised by one or even two.

The community first purchased the property on which Kahler Middle School sits on May 24, 1896, for the grand sum of two hundred dollars. Shortly thereafter, a two-room schoolhouse was erected that served the educational needs of the developing community for some years. However, with the passing of time, as the community continued to grow, the St. John School (as it was then called) was remodeled and refurbished time and again. Wings were added and removed until it reached its current form in 1996.

Touring the building, one cannot help but think of the countless geography lessons, spelling tests and math quizzes that have taken place on these grounds in the last 125 years. While time has wrought expansive changes to the school, one element that has remained unchanged is the dedication and passion of the teachers and staff to awakening young minds to the marvel of learning. In its history, Kahler has been blessed by a great many selfless and devoted teachers. None, however, has been so notable as Agnes Kahler, for whom the school is named.

Agnes Kahler began her teaching career in the community in 1917 at the age of twenty-six. For the next fifty-two years of her life, she tirelessly devoted herself to the education of young minds. While Miss Kahler never married and had no children of her own, to all those who were fortunate enough to have her as a teacher, she was both a friend and a role model.

As one former pupil (herself now a retired educator) remembers, "Educationally, Miss Kahler was well ahead of her time. Long before the advent of ideas like grouping children into teams for projects, Agnes was doing just that. She was a pioneer in educational models that are being used today."

However, according to all who knew her, Agnes Kahler's contribution to her students and community went far beyond her professional commitment. For more than half a century, the dauntless Miss Kahler poured herself personally into her work. As another former student fondly remembers, "Some people just pass in and out of your life and leave little behind them. Then there are those who share so much of themselves that they make an indelible mark on you for the

Photo: Chris Schultz

The grave of Agnes Kahler overlooking Kahler School, Dyer, Indiana.

rest of your life. Miss Kahler was that type of person. She just opened herself up to her students and her students were her life."

Another former schooladministrator, Kay Trapp, fondly remembers, "It was never a nine-to-five job for Agnes. She ministered to her students—she cared about their lives educationally and socially. It was an honor to work with her. There are people and there are *People,* and when you talk about Agnes Kahler, you capitalize it. She was one of the most outstanding, yet humble people I have ever met. "

In 1962 Agnes Kahler retired from active teaching. However, four years prior to her retirement, the Lake Central School Corporation honored her by naming the St. John Township School after her. It was a fitting tribute to a lady whose love had been the spirit of that school for so many years. After retirement, Miss Kahler moved to a home for retired Roman Catholic Nuns, where she died in 1983. It is both appropriate and touchingly significant that she was buried in the St. Joseph Cemetery, overlooking the school that she loved.

It can be truly said that the spirit of Agnes Kahler lives on in the lives that she touched and the school in which she invested herself. Countless adults today remember the venerable educator with fondness and appreciation. However, at least a few of those she left behind seem to wonder if Miss Kahler ever truly left the school that now bears her name. Indeed, if the events that have been rumored around the school for years are true, they well might have some cause to wonder.

One who tells the old tales of the school is Jean Wease, who was principal of Kahler Middle School from 1978 to 1993. Long before becoming principal of the school, however, Mrs. Wease was well acquainted with Agnes Kahler, having sat in her fifth grade class as a student many years before. Many years later, in the course of her duties as principal, Mrs. Wease was to hear a few odd stories that would give her pause.

"The first thing was about Miss Kahler's room. She had had the same room, a fifth grade class, for most of the time she was at the school," Jean remembers. "It was known to everybody as Miss Kahler's room."

"In 1970, after Agnes had been retired for some time, we did not need to use the entire building, so we moved the classes out of that part of the building. But then, in the mid 1980s, about the time of Miss Kahler's death, we got crowded again so we moved the students back in.

"When I moved the new teacher into Miss Kahler's room" Jean continues, "I took special pains to take her in and explain the room's significance—I thought it was special, owing to the history of that room. She thought it was neat, so she put a special plaque with a tribute to Agnes Kahler in her room. She framed the obituary that the paper had run on Agnes and hung it over the door. She took a great deal of pride in the fact that this had been Agnes' classroom."

A few months later, the teacher casually mentioned to Mrs. Wease that occasionally, while in the midst of teaching a lesson, the door to the room would open by itself, as though someone were entering. However, no one was in the hallway at the time. Seeking to make light of the event, the teacher would jokingly tell her class that Miss Kahler was coming in for a visit and would invite Miss Kahler to take a seat while the lesson continued. "It was odd," Jean Wease comments, "because none of the other doors in that building ever swung open. Just the doors in that hallway."

This seemingly minor series of events and the comment they elicited from the good-natured teacher would take on a larger significance in light of later events. One odd incident centered around the framed tribute to Agnes Kahler that hung in her classroom for many years. Eventually, with a shift in classrooms, a new teacher, Ms. Roxann Whitcombe, was moved into the classroom.

"One of the first days of summer, after the students were gone, I started moving my things into the classroom," Ms. Whitcombe now remembers. "In the process, I took the plaque down from where it hung over the door and put it on my desk, thinking that I would return it to the teacher who had left it there. After a while I left for lunch and locked the door behind me, but when I got back, the picture was gone from my desk. The door had been locked the entire time and there were no children there who might have taken it. We sent out notes asking if anyone had picked it up, but in all the years since then, it has never been found."

In subsequent years, the peculiar incidents seem to have followed Ms. Whitcombe even after she switched classrooms once again. She also reports that one school day in 1999, her teaching was disrupted when five books, which sat on the top shelf of a bookcase of her classroom, simultaneously launched themselves from the bookcase and landed several feet away. As odd as the incident seems, such occurrences are not unheard of in the halls of Kahler Middle School.

Mary Tanis, who has worked at the school for 27 years, also recalls several eerie experiences, beginning many years ago with a similar experience with the strange behavior of a door in the old annex hallway.

"Initially, I had a classroom in the old annex next door to the classroom where Agnes Kahler had taught for so many years." Mrs. Tanis recalls. "A lot of times I would be teaching and the door would open or shut by itself. In the old annex, the doors were solid and very heavy but sometimes, for no apparent reason, the door would shut all by itself. Then, at times when the door was shut, I would see the doorknob turn and the door would open, but no one was there."

Mary also recalls times when the hanging plants in her room would suddenly start to spin in a circle for no apparent reason. "I guess you could write that off to an air current from the heating system except that it would happen when the heating system was not on and even if it was, I can't understand why it would make the plants start swinging in a perfect circle."

An even more eerie report regarding the room formerly occupied by Agnes Kahler came to the ear of former Principal Dr. Nikki Tsangaris from some of her custodial staff. It seems that one night, while alone in that part of the building, one of the staff was waxing the floor in the hallway outside Ms. Kahler's former classroom. Completing his task, the staff member moved from the hallway to pursue other jobs in the building.

In a few hours, however, as he returned to check on his work, the worker was shocked to find a set of footprints in the fresh wax leading from Miss Kahler's classroom to the stairs. What made this finding doubly curious was that the footprints stopped in the middle of the hallway, a few feet short of the stairway. By all appearances, the person who had left them had made her way toward the stairs, only to vanish before reaching them.

Indeed, the custodial staff seems to have been witness to more than a few odd goings on at the school. Garland Lauderdale, who worked in the school as head custodian from 1988 to 1997, remembers many such inexplicable events.

"You would walk through an area, especially one of the older sections of the building, and you would just catch a glimpse of something—a shadow moving maybe, or you would hear an odd noise and you would just get the feeling that you were not alone." Mr. Lauderdale reports. "A few months after I started working I was talking to my supervisor and happened to comment, 'there are a lot of weird things that happen here!' His response to me was 'So you have had a taste of those too, huh?' "

In the years that Garland spent at the school, he seems to have gotten more than a taste of odd events there. "You would be waxing the hallways and you would hear something walking through the building, even though you knew the doors were locked and you were alone. Lights would go on and off by themselves, other staff would tell me about hearing footsteps or voices…it got to be a regular thing."

"When I was made head custodian," Mr. Lauderdale continues, "I had staff come to me and tell me that they would not work alone in the building. One woman we had working in an upstairs classroom said that she was cleaning the floor once when all of a sudden a projector screen pulled itself out from the wall and then folded up and flipped off the wall. She was really spooked."

Garland Lauderdale also remembers hearing from another employee who seemed upset by the happenings she encountered in the annex section of the building. "I had another young woman who came in and worked as a substitute custodian that came to me one night and said that she would not work alone in the upper level of the B Annex. When I asked her why, she told me that while she was alone up there she was constantly hearing footsteps, lights would go on and off, and once her vacuum cleaner turned itself on when she was several feet away from it."

Mr. Lauderdale himself also experienced several odd incidents in the building. "One Sunday afternoon my wife and son and I were in the building and as we walked through the halls I could hear desks moving in one classroom. I was afraid that someone had broken into the school but when we got there, the sounds had stopped, the door was locked and no one was in the room. However several desks had been knocked over and one was tilted sideways against the wall. There was no way anyone could have gotten in or out of that room without me knowing it."

Mr. Lauderdale also reports that one end of the upper hall of the annex was sometimes noted to be abnormally cold. "There was no reason why that area should have a different temperature than the rest of the building or even the rest of that floor. The heating system was working perfectly but it was always colder there," Garland remembers. "One time we took a thermometer down there to test it and it registered a fifteen-degree difference from the rest of the hallway."

One of the most evocative occurrences, however, happened one winter night when Mr. Lauderdale, then head custodian, was home enjoying an evening off. His peace was disturbed by a phone call from one his staff working at the building, who advised him to come over right away, saying only he and another custodian "had something to show him."

Somewhat reluctantly, Garland left his home and drove through several inches of new fallen snow to Kahler Middle School, parking his car and entering through the main entrance. "I got there and they took me through the hallway to the back of the school and carefully unlocked the back door," he now recalls. Pushing the door open against the snow that had drifted against it, the custodian pointed to the empty parking lot and said, "See the footprints?"

A set of footprints across the new snow did indeed lead across the parking lot to the door that had just been unlocked. However, what made these particular footprints unique were that, though they led to a door that had been locked and chained, they only led one way. It was readily apparent that had someone tried to gain access to the school only to find themselves locked out, they would have had to turn and retrace their steps. In this case, however, the footsteps simply led to the door and stopped.

Yet, as Mr. Lauderdale stood staring into the cold night air, an even more haunting and significant aspect to these phantom footsteps also became apparent. As Garland traced the course of the strange footprints, his eyes traced their path to their origin. As he recalls today, they led across the parking lot and on into St. Joseph cemetery where Agnes Kahler had been laid to rest years before.

Interestingly, while Mr. Lauderdale is hesitant to say that he believes the spirit of the beloved teacher still walks the halls of Kahler School, he is far more convinced that another phantom might reside there: the phantom of a child, whose origins are unknown.

"We definitely had a boy there," Garland says. "We heard him and saw him. Once we had waxed the cafeteria floor one afternoon after school. When we were done, we locked the doors to the cafeteria and in fact locked up the whole school. But the next morning I got a call from the school asking me why I had waxed the floor and then walked across it. I got to the school and sure enough, there were footprints in the wax—but this time, they were a child's footprints. I asked the staff if the doors had been locked when they got there and they said they had, so there was no way anyone could have gotten in or out of that cafeteria. It could not have happened."

However, this was not to be the only time when evidence of a ghostly child would be found in the building. Garland Lauderdale reports that both he and other custodians would see the phantom boy all through the building. "He always looked the same," Garland reflects. "He had on jeans, a striped shirt and a sweater. I saw him several times and chased him, but neither I nor anyone else could catch him. He would turn down a hallway that you knew was locked on the other end and you would follow him, but he would be gone. The door at the other end could not have been opened and we searched every room, but he was gone."

If Mr. Lauderdale and the other staff members still thought their visitor was of flesh and blood, such thoughts were erased one night when he and two other custodians were working in the gymnasium area. "We were working on the floor in the gym one night when one of the guys looked up and saw this kid just standing there staring at us. When my coworker said something to us, we all looked up and the kid turned and ran into the locker room. Now there are only two entrances to that locker room, both through the gym and there is no place to hide, so I thought to myself, 'Now we have him!'

"I ran to one entrance and told the other custodian to go in by the other entrance. We could hear the sounds of locker doors slamming, like someone was running past them, but when we got in the locker room, there was absolutely no one there. It was impossible, but let me tell you it happened." By now disturbed by their late night visitor, the men quickly concluded their work in the gymnasium and left that part of the building.

Another common element to the stories told of Kahler School deal with electrical devices that seem to turn themselves off and on of their own volition, sometimes regardless of whether or not power is supplied to them. Garland Lauderdale reports several instances when lights that had been previously turned off have been found on, despite the fact that their switches are still found in the off position.

Another such story is told by Dr. Tsangaris, the former principal. "A few years ago, on the day after students had left for the summer, I was visiting with Roxann Whitcombe in the commons area of the pod where she worked. I remember it was a really hot day and they had fans going in the commons area. Everyone else had already left, so after talking for a while, she picked up her stuff and we turned off the fan and walked to the stairs."

However, just before descending the stairs, both women were surprised to hear the sound of the fan running again. Somewhat bewildered, they turned to the commons area to find that the fan had indeed turned itself on once again and was running, despite the fact that the switch was clearly turned off. "We just sort of looked at each other for a minute and then unplugged the fan from the wall and left quickly," Dr. Tsangaris recalls.

Such an incident, reported alone, might sound like the minor malfunction of an appliance. When taken together with the other reports, however, it causes one to wonder at the eerie and inexplicable pattern that emerges.

Since 1993, when the older annex (which seems to have been the site of many of the strange occurrences) was torn down, the reports of spectral activities seem to have died down considerably. However, seemingly inexplicable events are still known to have occurred since that time. Garland Lauderdale recalls such a time, shortly before he left the school in 1997. As he now relates, he was talking with other staff members in the office area of the building, when all present distinctly heard the sound of the door to the copy room open and close. "We walked to the room and one of us said, 'Can we help you?' expecting someone to be there, but the whole area was empty. The door was closed and locked."

As recently as the fall of 2000, teachers have reported several strange incidents. Mary Tanis reports one odd episode that occurred in the first week of September. "It was during the day as I was teaching class. I remember that there was a computer technician there working on the classroom computer," Mrs. Tanis says. "We were going about our business when suddenly the clock in the classroom flew off the wall and landed six feet away. It did not simply fall off the wall—it flew off with enough force to pull the wire out of the wall. The computer tech worker stopped what he was doing and the kids looked at me wide-eyed. I just smiled and said, 'Don't worry, it's just Agnes,' and we went on as if nothing had happened."

A week or so later, Ms. Whitcombe experienced a similar event in her classroom. "In my classroom I have a small slate board that generally is propped up on the ledge under my black board. As I was teaching suddenly this slate board just flew off the ledge and landed two feet away. Neither I nor any of my students were near it when it happened. It was just a little spooky."

If indeed the spirit of the beloved Agnes Kahler or the mysterious phantom of a child does still roam the halls of Kahler School, no one there seems to be concerned. "It is not a scary, spooky sort of story," Jean Wease reflects. "I always thought that if it was Agnes, that was sort of a good thing. Agnes loved this school and the students here and maybe in some way her spirit is still here."

Nikki Tsangaris agrees. "Do I think the school is haunted?" she sagely reflects, "Yes and no. I believe that people's spirits do transcend their bodies. I would like to think that my father and grandma are here now…and so I do believe that Agnes is among us. I don't believe in scary kind of haunts, however. To me it must be more peaceful than that...something gentle and even loving."

Gentle and loving are words that seem to encompass the spirit of Agnes Kahler. Perhaps that spirit is nothing more than a sweet memory in the minds of her former pupils and the legacy of selfless dedication that she left to her fellow teachers. Yet the tales of the spirits of Kahler School do remain, handed down from generation to generation among the students and staff of this proud educational facility. These are stories of a dedicated and loving teacher who still maintains a spirited interest in her school, and perhaps of a young boy who joins her in her late night rambles.

8

A FEW HISTORIC GHOSTS OF THE INDIANA LAKE REGION

North Central Indiana[8]

"While yet a boy, I sought for ghosts, and sped through many a listening chamber, cave and ruin and starlit wood with fearful steps pursuing hopes of high talk with the departed dead."

Percy Bysshe Shelley

In honesty, Indiana is not widely known as a haven for sun and water sports. Ask the average individual what areas of the United States they think of in relation to aquatic recreation and they will probably mention the beaches of Florida, California, or perhaps the fabled "ten thousand lakes" of Minnesota. Yet in truth, Indiana can boast of a great number of recreational lakes and reservoirs. From the famed quarry swimming in Bloomington to the fishing in the Missesinewa Reservoir, Indiana offers an opportunity to while away a summer afternoon on many impressive bodies of water.

No area in the state, however, is so noted as the lakes region of Kosciusko County. Located in north central Indiana, just a short drive from South Bend to the north and Fort Wayne to the east, this gently rolling countryside offers no less than fifty-three lakes. Moreover, unlike other areas noted for their summer recreation, this area has been slow to give in to the rush of overcommercialization. While in the summer months, the area does experience a vast influx of weekend residents and vacationers, still it remains unspoiled and scenic. In the small towns that dot the region, such as Warsaw, North Webster, and Pierceton, one can still relax in quaint, wholesome surroundings.

The area is also rich in history. Well over a century ago, entrepreneurs realizing the near-idyllic conditions of the remote location and inviting lakes of the region began to develop resort hotels and rental properties along the lakes. While most of the large hotels have disappeared today, for many years until the 1930s, these establishments attracted a host of visitors from across the state and country. As will be noted, these guests included some of the most famous and infamous personalities of their time.

Considering that history, it is understandable that with the passage of time the lakes region has also begun to assemble a series of ghostly tales as well. Some are of a more prosaic nature. At least one cottage on Webster Lake is said to be inhabited by the spirit of a former owner who rattles pots in the kitchen in the morning and who has been known to douse cigarettes left unattended in ashtrays. (Since a church camp once owned the cottage in question, such behavior must

Photo: Mark Marimen

Merbrink, on the shores of Winona Lake.

be excused.) As fascinating and disconcerting as these manifestations are to the current occupants of the cottage, however, to the avid ghost story aficionado they are merely the bread and butter of supernatural legends.

However, at least two locations can boast of more historic and, at least in one case, famous spirits. Theirs are stories that transcend time and even, it is believed, life and death itself.

Once such spirit, who has become a bit of a local celebrity, is a mysterious phantom known to the local residents as "Miss Phoebe." Her home is a majestic mansion called "Merbrink" in the small town of Winona Lake.

The community of Winona Lake was developed primarily as a site for Christian camps and conferences. The first of these began in 1895 when Dr. Sol C. Dickey began the Winona Lake Bible Conference outside of Warsaw. Soon, hundreds and then thousands of christians from across the state and the midwest were streaming to the shores of Winona Lake each summer for week long revivals.

Soon, a second Christian conference, the Chautauqua Conference, was instituted, and the crowds grew each summer for learning, worship, and to hear world renowned evangelists, especially the famous Rev. Billy Sunday, the most fiery and charismatic speaker of his day. Reverend Sunday became a regular fixture in the growing community, eventually making Winona Lake his headquarters and building a home nearby.

During the heyday of the Bible conferences, in the early 1900s it is said that as many as ten thousand people each week would travel by train to Winona Lakes, and soon a whole community sprung up around the lake to meet the needs of the faithful. Restaurants, summer cottages, and a variety of inns and hotels grew around the conference grounds.

By the mid 1930s, the popularity of the conferences held at Winona Lake had declined, and they were discontinued. However, by then the community itself was well established, augmented by Grace College, a Christian educational facility that had been founded some years earlier. Time has wrought its changes on the community, yet it retains much of its bygone charm and character.

One thing that has not changed at Winona Lake is the stately home perched along the shore called Merbrink. This is the name given to it by its builder, William Bruning, nearly a hundred years ago. For many years, it was known to the local residents of Winona Lake as "the mystery house." As such, the home has been the source of much speculation and the center of many local tales and legends.

The history of the house itself has been the subject of legend, much of it inaccurate. No less a personage than the Rev. Billy Sunday himself referred to it in one of his many sermons delivered at the Winona Lake Christian Assembly campgrounds. Speaking in the early 1900s, Sunday remarked:

> Nothing happens by chance. We are put here for a purpose. I know of a house by the lake, beautifully furnished for a bride. But the girl changed her mind and it still stands there, all boarded up. The furniture is still in that unoccupied house, dust covered.

In his remarks, the venerable Reverend Sunday was relating the popular belief regarding the history of Merbrink. Indeed, the story is still told today in the area that the home was built by a groom for his prospective bride who then jilted him at the altar. According to the tale, the groom, heartbroken, boarded up the home and refused to enter the house he had so lavishly provided for his lover.

This tale of unrequited love is truly a classic, romantic tale. However like many such legends, it does not match up with historical facts. The real story of Merbrink began in the early days of Winona Lake's development, with a man named William Brunning. Brunning, a wealthy import-export dealer from Evansville, as well as a devout Christian, was an active member of the Christian Association that developed and ran the Winona Lake campgrounds. As an astute man of business, Brunning also realized the commercial opportunities created by the thousands of visitors brought to the area by the evangelical meetings each year. In the early days of the last century, he opened the Swiss Terrace, a boarding house near the Winona Lake camp. Each summer Brunning would travel from his home in Evansville to attend the camp meetings and oversee the operations of his hotel.

As time passed, Brunning became well acquainted with other hotel operators in the small community, including the Cooper family.

Mr. and Mrs. Cooper, along with their daughter Nelly, had been hired to run the Winona Inn, the largest hotel in the area. Such was his respect for the family that after several years, with the death of Mr. Cooper, when Nelly and her mother found themselves displaced from their employment at the Winona Inn, Brunning hired the pair to run his Swiss Terrace.

Perhaps by the time he brought Nelly Cooper into his employ, Brunning, a lifelong bachelor, was already developing feelings for her that went beyond professional respect. What is known is that within a few years of her coming to the Swiss Terrace, Brunning and Nelly had developed a deep mutual devotion for one another. In 1905, Brunning proposed marriage and Nelly joyfully accepted. As a wedding present to his perspective bride, he built her the beautiful and gracious home known as Merbrink, so called due to its proximity to the clear waters of Winona Lake.

In a happier tale, this might have been the beginning of a love story—but it is not. Before the pair could be wed, Nelly's mother became ill. Despite her love for her fiancé, Nelly Cooper felt an even greater loyalty to and responsibility for her mother. Ms. Cooper reluctantly told her beloved William she could not marry him until the time when her mother's health had resolved itself. Certainly, this blow had to have been a grievous one for Brunning, yet he resolved to wait for his beloved Nelly no matter how long it took.

It would turn out to be a fateful promise. As it turned out, it would take nearly fifteen years and the death of Nelly's mother before the two would walk to the alter. During that time, the beautiful home called Merbrink sat empty and boarded up. Each spring, workers hired by Brunning would come to the house, take the boards from the windows and doors, thoroughly clean and air the house, and then replace the boards for another year.

In the early 1920s, William Brunning and Nelly Cooper were finally married, By then, William was in his late fifties and his bride just a few years younger than he, yet the couple was as happy as any blushing newlyweds could be. At last, after so many years of waiting, they could share their lives, as well as their summer home of Merbrink, together.

Even after Nelly and William were married, however, their time at Merbrink proved tragically short. For two or three golden years, the pair would travel from their home in Evansville to their Winona Lakes home to spend their summers. During that time, Nelly grew to love the home in which she had yearned to live for so long. However, just a few short years after their marriage, Nelly Cooper fell ill and was unable to make the their annual trip from Evansville to Winona Lake. Once more the home was boarded up.

Eventually, Nelly Cooper died in Evansville, never returning to the home she had dreamed of for so many years. A short time later, her husband followed her in death. Since the couple had been childless, the home, Merbrink, was left to a nephew of William Brunning's in Los Angeles, who showed no interest in owning a home half way across the country. For years the house was left to fall into disrepair until it was repossessed by the county for back taxes.

In 1931 the home was sold by the county to Mr. Donald White and his wife. Mrs. White had grown up in the Winona Lakes area, and had long been in love with the decrepit house and the romantic tales told of it. She and her husband, a renowned college basketball coach at Washington University and Rutgers University, used Merbrink for their summer residence for many years. Here their two daughters grew up, idling away the golden summer afternoons swimming in the waters of Winona Lake and hiking in the nearby woods.

With the death of Mr. White, Merbrink passed into the hands of their daughter, Anna Lou Stewart, who owns the home today. Under her loving care and that of her three sons, the venerable old mansion has been restored to its original splendor. Today the once neglected edifice stands as a beautiful testament to the history of the surrounding community.

It is only natural that such a place, with its history of romance and tragedy, would become the focus of rumors and legends in the community. Indeed, for many years, tales have been told of its past and in particular, the possibility of ghostly inhabitants in the home. However, unlike many such tales, according to Anna Stewart there may be more to at least some of them than mere legend.

"For as long as I can remember, this house was called 'the haunted house' by the kids in the neighborhood," she says. "I think some of the stories began when the house was boarded up all of those years. Another possibility was related to the fact that Nelly Cooper was said to have loved to play the harp and at one time there was a leaded window on the second floor that supposedly had harp strings actually worked into the glass. When the wind blew, you could hear what sounded like a harp playing and that lead to the rumor that the ghost of Nelly was playing in the house."

Such a rational explanation accounts for some of the stories of the home, yet certainly not all. As Ms. Stewart goes on to say, other tales of ghostly phenomena at the house are not so easily explained away.

"We always called the ghost 'Miss Phoebe,' " Ms. Stewart says. "When we first moved into the house, everybody mentioned Miss Phoebe and I never understood how she got the name. We never really thought about the ghost until one morning an incident happened with my dad that really made us think."

As Anna tells the story, one summer morning when the family was vacationing at the home, her father, an avid fisherman, rose before the rest of the family and took a small boat onto the lake to fish. As the sun rose above the waters of Winona Lake, Mr. White, anchored just off the point on which Merbrink stands, happened to glance up at the screened-in sleeping porch off the master bedroom on the second floor. He saw the figure of a woman in a white gown, standing and looking out peacefully toward the water. Thinking that his wife had risen early, he waved to the figure who, he later said, waved back.

Later, after returning to the home, Mr. White found his wife in the kitchen and asked her if she had experienced trouble sleeping. After being assured that she had slept well, he next asked his wife why she had been out on the sleeping porch at such an early hour. To his surprise, his wife reported that she had risen only a short time before and had not been on the sleeping porch that morning.

"That," says Anna Stewart, "was the first time we began to think that there was something more to the stories than just rumors."

Indeed, in the next several years, there would be more and more evidence that the family shared their beautiful home with an otherworldly presence.

"One night when my sister and I were in high school," she recalls, "my parents went out for the evening and my sister and I started talking about Miss Phoebe. We decided that we would have a séance to conjure her up, but for some reason we decided that to do a séance, we had to burn incense. Well, we turned the house upside down but we could not find any of the incense that my mother normally kept around. When we could not find any, we abandoned the idea of a séance and went on to other things.

"Well, later that night, my parents got home and when my mother stepped into the house she said, 'Where did you find incense? The whole house smells of it!' My sister and I told her we had looked for incense but had not found any, yet my mother swore that she smelled incense all throughout the house."

Perhaps, as Ms. Stewart conjectures, Miss. Phoebe was attempting to tell their mother what the sisters had been up to in her absence. In any case, this was not the only instance of strange incidents in the house. Many have continued to this day.

"Sometimes I feel that I am not alone," Ms. Stewart adds. "Quite often when I have been away from the house, I come back and I feel strongly that she is welcoming me. I always say, 'Well, I'm back and it looks pretty good —looks like you took care of the place.' "

At moments, whatever seems to occupy the home has gone beyond the mere feeling of a presence. In at least once case, Miss Phoebe has shown her feelings about the décor in the home.

"I have a collection of dolls," Ms. Stewart says, "and over the years, I have collected dolls from all across the world. A couple of years ago, I decided to display the dolls so I put them on a shelf in one of the bedrooms that we call 'the children's room.' The next morning I came in and found one of the dolls on the floor at least twenty feet from the shelf. It could not have fallen off the shelf and even if it had, it would have broken. I could not understand it, but I put the doll back on the shelf. The next morning, there she was again—across the room from where I had left her. It happened two or three times, until I decided that Miss Phoebe did not want the dolls there. So I moved them to another bedroom and they have been fine ever since."

The sequel to this story came one evening in the spring of 2000, when Ms. Stewart and her son were entertaining guests in the house. As the evening wore on, the talked turned to the ghost of Merbrink and Anna's son, Kevin, laughingly told the friends the story of the dolls. He concluded by jokingly suggesting that an errant breeze had somehow picked up the doll and deposited it across the room.

"At the time, we all laughed about it and then the conversation moved on," Anna says. "But the next morning, Kevin was walking past his bedroom where I had put the dolls several years before and there was that same doll lying on the bed that he usually slept on."

Kevin also reports strange happenings in the home. "One November, my brother and I were finishing up putting a new foundation on the house. My mother was away on an extended trip and so that last day when we were finishing up the foundation, we were also closing up the house. We stored everything away and then put plastic sheets on the mattresses to protect them. Just before we left the house for the winter we did a final walk-through. When we were up in the children's bedroom where I sleep now, suddenly a wind whipped through the room. All the windows were shut tight but as we stood there, this breeze just sort of came from nowhere. It was strong enough to move the pictures on the wall and took the plastic right off of the beds. We both got chills and left. Thinking back on it, I tend to think that Miss Phoebe did not want us to leave the house. She did not want to see the place shut up again."

Interestingly, while the fame of Miss Phoebe has spread throughout the Winona Lake community, no one seems to know just where the name came from. In searching through the historical records of the place, Anna Stewart has been unable to find any mention of anyone by that name ever having lived in the home.

"The only hint I had was one night when I was a little girl and my parents took my sister and me out to dinner at a restaurant in town. We started talking to a local family there and someone asked us if we were scared sharing the house with Miss Phoebe. When we said we weren't, one of the older women at the table turned to us and said very seriously, 'You shouldn't be scared. Phoebe was one of the nicest ladies you could ever meet—she would never hurt anyone!' "

Looking back at the conversation now, Anna reflects, "I wish I would have asked the lady who Phoebe was, but back then children did not ask questions of adults. But that is the only indication I have ever had that there might actually have been someone named Phoebe who was attached to Merbrink."

Whoever, or whatever, may reside within the walls of Merbrink, tales of her presence have filtered through the community for many years. However much her presence has been felt there, she has been seen only twice. The first sighting came, as mentioned above, to Anna's father, when he glimpsed a figure on the second floor sleeping porch. The second sighting came about a decade ago, in a very similar manner.

Anna recalls, "In 1990, a man who is sort of the informal town historian was taking pictures around the town and was snapping pictures of the outside of our house. As he did so, he saw someone who he thought was me on the sleeping porch outside my bedroom and they exchanged waves. Later, when he developed the pictures, he was shocked to see that the person had not shown up in the pictures. He came to me and showed me the pictures and I had to explain to him that I had not been on the porch that day—I had been downstairs all afternoon and had not been anywhere near the sleeping porch."

Perhaps, as some have surmised, it was the spirit of the elusive Miss Phoebe, the mysterious and gentle presence who has made herself a part of the mansion known as Merbrink for many years. Her identity forever obscured through the passage of time, she has still left an indelible mark on the community of Winona Lakes.

* * *

While the fame of Miss Phoebe is well known throughout her Winona Lake community, she is by no means the only spectral resident of the Indiana Lakes region. Just a few miles from Winona Lakes there stands an old hotel that can boast of yet another historical guest who, it is said, has left something of himself behind long after his mortal existence has "checked out."

Sitting on Barbee Lake, (and the adjacent "Barbee Chain" of lakes) the Barbee Hotel appears at first glance like simply an attractive, upscale restaurant and inn. Indeed, the facility itself is exudes a comfortable elegance that is in keeping with the serenity of its surroundings. While the hotel itself is certainly impressive, what is most remarkable about the facility is its history—a history that spans over one hundred years and features a cast of characters that spasn the range of the famous to the infamous.

The history of the Barbee Hotel can be traced to 1897, when local resident Charles Ormond built an inn on the shores of Barbee Lake to cater to the plethora of sportsmen and fishermen who swarmed to the area each summer to fish the pristine waters of the Lakes region and to hunt in the woods that still blanketed the area. Called the Ormond Hotel, the name of the inn was later changed to the Barbee Hotel, in honor of William Barbee, one of the original settlers to the area.

Business was good from the start. Despite (or perhaps because of) the remote location of the inn, there were plenty of fishermen willing to travel by rail to Warsaw, the nearest city, and then endure a half day carriage ride to Barbee Lake and the other waters attached to it. Visitors from such rapidly developing settlements as Chicago, Indianapolis, and Fort Wayne came to enjoy the rustic surroundings and the fish and game they provided.

By the early decades of the twentieth century, the popularity of the Barbee Hotel grew with the advent of the automobile. However, the history of the hotel was nearly obliterated in 1922, when the inn was destroyed by fire. The next year Mr. and Mrs. C. L. Lincoln of Indianapolis purchased the land and rebuilt the hotel, and once again the fortunes of the Barbee soared.

By the mid 1920s, the horse-drawn carriages carrying visitors to the hotel were replaced by a stream of sedans and black limousines, carrying within them some of the most colorful characters of the time. In those dark days of prohibition, it was no longer simply sportsmen who came to the Lakes region, but also notorious gangsters as well. Seeking refuge from the large cities that served as the base of their operations, such gangsters sought out the area to elude both law enforcement and rival gangs when "things got hot." When visiting the lakes region, they sought out the comparative comfort of the Barbee Hotel. Such colorful names as John Dillinger, "Baby Face" Nelson, and Al Capone, "King of the Gangsters," were all known to be guests of the inn during this period of time.

In particular, the Barbee Hotel seems to have been a favorite hideout of Capone, according to local history. In a newspaper interview several years ago, one longtime resident recalled watching as a line of long black limousines pulling up to the front of the hotel, disgorging lines of men in black suits carrying ominous-looking oblong cases, as might be used to transport machine guns. According to local history, as gang warfare raged in Chicago, it was common for ordinary residents of the second floor rooms in the hotel to be informed that they were to be moved to surrounding cottages, as the entire second floor was to be rented to "an important out of town guest." It was also about that time that iron shutters were installed on the second floor windows that could have afforded a measure of protection in case of incoming gunfire.

In many other locations, such stories might easily be relegated to the realm of local folklore, but in the case of the Barbee Hotel, sound historical evidence linking the presence of Capone with the inn is well established, both by historical records and by the recollections of many former residents of the area.

However, the presence of Al Capone and his cohorts in crime was

Photo courtesy of Barbee Hotel

Ormond Hotel, on the site of the current Barbee Hotel, circa 1900.

not the only time the Barbee Hotel would play host to guests of notoriety. This time, however, it was not the world of crime, but rather the glittering world of Hollywood that would provide the Barbee Hotel's brush with greatness.

It was in 1939, long after the passage of the gangster era, that Carole Lombard and Clark Gable came to spend a portion of their honeymoon at the Barbee Hotel. Interestingly, it was not the first time Lombard had visited the area. A native of Fort Wayne, Lombard had spent several summers as a young girl at Barbee Lake, where her uncle had a cottage. By 1939, when Lombard, by then one of America's shining stars, wed the equally famous Gable, they decided on a honeymoon spot far from the crowds and notoriety of Hollywood. Remembering her tranquil youth in the Indiana Lakes region, she suggested it as a suitable getaway.

After a private wedding in Arizona, the pair were quietly flown to Indianapolis, from which they traveled by car to the Barbee Hotel. After staying in what is now known as the "Gable and Lombard Suite," the pair rented a nearby cottage for the rest of their stay in the area.

Photo courtesy of Barbee Hotel

Barbee Hotel as it appears today.

With their stay, the two stars forever sealed the fame of the Barbee Hotel in local lore and history.

With the passing of time, the ownership of Barbee Hotel changed hands numerous times and the fortunes of the hotel seemed to decline. By the early 1960s, the guest rooms were closed and the hotel reverted to a restaurant. However, in 1992 the property was purchased by its current owner, Phil Fozo, who renovated the hotel inside and out and reopened the third floor rooms to guests. Today, under Fozo's continued entrepreneurial direction, the hotel is once more busy and prosperous, with full dining and banquet facilities, as well as ten guest rooms. Touring the inn today, with pictures of its vaunted history decorating the walls around, one cannot escape the impression that this is a place where the past and present are intermingled in a delicate and gracious balance.

Perhaps it is this very balance that in some way accounts for the fact that, as some believe, some portions of the past are still very active in the hotel—guests who might possibly have stayed on beyond their required checkout time.

Phil Fozo tells many such stories. More than a few seem to center around the third floor where many guests, including Mr. Capone, have stayed over the years. "The first thing I really encountered was nothing more than a smell," Mr. Fozo relates, warming to his story. "When I bought the place I had not really heard of any spooky stories, but shortly after I purchased the hotel in '92, I had a housekeeper come to me and say that she had smelled a cigar odor in the hallway outside of one particular room—Room 316. That is one of the rooms where they say Capone stayed. Anyway, the first time I heard it, I just sort of ignored it, but after the first several months a couple more of the staff, a few of whom did not know each other, came to me with the same story. I even went up there and I could smell it too. The odd thing was that in each case the room had been vacant the night before, but the smell was definitely there."

Mr. Fozo adds, "Then one of my staff, Becky, came to me and said that she had seen a faint haze at the end of one of the hallways. It was like a small area of fog that drifted across the end of one hall. Then other girls started seeing it too. It was strange to say the least."

Interestingly, Mr. Fozo was not terribly upset by the possibility that something inexplicable might be occurring in the hotel he had just purchased. "Before I moved to this area I had lived in a place I am convinced was haunted," he says with a wry smile, "so I guess that this did not upset me. I just did not think about it all that much." However, as Mr. Fozo continued to work in and around the hotel, more and more incidents intruded into his life there.

"My office is on the third floor and within the first couple of months I started hearing noises from the rooms at the end of the hall," he reflects. "It sounded like a party going on—you could not tell exactly where the sounds were coming from, but when I would leave my office and walk toward the general direction, the noises would just fade away. This happened sometimes in the early morning, when I was alone up there and sometimes at night as well.

"Then, one morning, I had a really strange experience in the bar area" Mr. Fozo continues. "I came in really early and I was the only one in the hotel. I was kneeling down behind the bar, working on a condenser in one of the coolers, when I heard the sound of the bar stools moving across the floor. It is an incredibly distinctive sound— you can't mistake it and I knew what I was hearing. But when I popped up from behind the bar, none of the stools had been touched. I was not more than three feet from them and I know for a fact what I heard, but there they sat. So, I just went about my business and tried to forget it."

However, perhaps Mr. Fozo's most memorable experience with the odd goings on in the place came when he caught a glimpse of the enigmatic fog that had been described to him by his employees.

As he now recalls, one afternoon, shortly after purchasing the hotel, he was on the third floor inspecting several rooms when something strange caught his eye at the far end of the hallway. As he turned, he saw what he describes as a smoky haze seeming to linger several feet above the floor. Thinking at first that there was a fire, Mr. Fozo rushed toward the end of the hall, only to have the smoke disappear as he approached it. Of course, no fire was found and a check revealed that all the smoke detectors in the hallway were operational. What makes this incident particularly significant is the fact that as Mr. Fozo reached the place in the hall where he had seen the hazy presence, he realized it had been located outside Room 316, just where the house-keeping staff had reported smelling the oder of cigar smoke.

These strange occurrences have continued throughout the eight years Mr. Fozo has owned the venerable establishment. "It might go for a month or two and nothing will happen, and then suddenly it starts up again—over a period of a month you will have four or five people report things," he says.

According to Mr. Fozo, guests and employees at the hotel have reported a variety of strange occurrences. "Several times I have had guests come to me in the morning and complain about how noisy the people staying two rooms down from them were, when I knew that they were the only guests staying in the hotel that night."

Other guests have reported hearing odd noises and rustlings coming from rooms that were apparently empty. One group of ladies who had come to the Barbee Hotel for a summer weekend reported hearing the sounds of moaning emanating from an empty room on the third floor late at night. Employees have continued to report the smell of cigar smoke coming from the area of Room 316, and more than one has also reported walking through strange "cold spots" in the third floor hallway as well. "These were not just drafts they described to me," Fozo says. "They were contained areas of intense cold."

Des Statler, who has worked at the hotel for the last three years, also reports a feeling of intense cold inside another room on the third floor. "In the dead heat of summer it gets real hot on the third floor, but I have walked into Room 311 and found it ice cold. One time I even got our bookkeeper to come up there with me. I did not tell her what I was doing, but I made her walk through several rooms and then when we got to Room 311 she said 'why is it so cold in here?' We both felt that there was something in that room and we got out of there quickly after that."

Ms. Statler also reports having seen some strange things while working at the hotel. "The first time was when I was vacuuming on the third floor—there is a stairway at the end of the hall down to the second floor and across the front of the second floor is a sunroom. I was vacuuming the stairway and I saw something cross between me and the light, so I looked up and saw the back part of a black jacket and leg—the rest of the body was cut off from my view by the stair-well. I knew I was supposed to be alone in the building so I went down to the sunroom, but there was no one there at all. In fact, just as I had thought, I was alone in the building. I was spooked—spooked but not scared."

This would not be the only time Ms. Statler would see something inexplicable at the Barbee. "One morning I was walking up to the hotel to come to work" she now recalls, "and I happened to glance up at the second floor window and there was a young man standing there. I could see he was in his twenties or early thirties and he had on an old-fashioned white shirt. He was staring down at me as I walked up toward the building and it was a little unnerving. When I got into the hotel there were only five people in the building and I immediately asked 'Who was that guy upstairs?' Somebody said 'You're nuts—there is no one upstairs!' To be sure, we all went up and searched, but there was no one else in the building."

Ms. Statler is not alone in her sightings of strange figures at the hotel. According to employees there, one guest from Chicago came downstairs one early morning with a strange and unsettling tale. He reported being awakened at 3 A.M. by a sound coming from the hall-way outside his room. Rising from his rest to investigate, the man opened the door to find himself face to face with a large man in a suit that he described as being from the 1930s. Understandably, the man quickly shut and locked his door and returned to his bed. According to the staff member whom he spoke with, "The man thought it was Al Capone, up walking the halls. He described the guy as having 'one ugly mug!' "

Whether or not the spirit of the infamous gangster does wander the halls of this wonderful old hotel will remain a matter of conjec-ture. In the end, it can never be proved that his spirit, or any other, truly resides within the walls of this century-old inn. However, like the spirit of Miss Phoebe, who is said to haunt the beautiful home known as Merbrink, the spirits of the Barbee Hotel are a part of the color and charm of the Indiana Lakes Region.

9
A HOOSIER BANSHEE
Batesville, Indiana[9]

"What beckoning ghost along the moonlight shade
Invites my steps, and points to yonder glade?"
       —Alexander Pope, "To the Memory of an Unfortunate Lady"

If the pages of this volume prove anything, hopefully they prove that Indiana ghosts are hardly a stereotypical lot. Instead of being confined by the ghostly peer conventions of shaking chains and disembodied bed sheets, Hoosier spirits come in a variety of characters and temperaments. From ethereal teachers who have never given up their posts to the shades of the famous and infamous, from cosmopolitan hitchhiking ghosts to rustic phantoms relegated to rural churchyards, the ghosts of our beloved state are nearly as varied and diverse a group as the corporeal residents of the region.

However, one common denominator to nearly all Indiana ghosts can be summed up in one word: *location*. This is to say that the vast majority of Indiana ghosts (like the spectral populace of the entire nation) are tied to specific locations. Of course, such a statement might be considered a matter of course for those well acquainted with ghostlore. Whether a gloomy mansion or a modern skyscraper, nearly all ghosts seem attached to a specific setting. Sometimes it is the site of their untimely demise, or perhaps a setting where they whiled away their earthly existence, but the rule for most ghosts seems to be the same as that for real estate: *location, location, location!*

Of course, for every rule there is bound to be an exception. Rarely, one does encounter a tale of a ghost who is not tied to a specific geographical setting. Author Ed Okonowicz, in his recent book, *Possessed Possessions,* has collected tales of ghosts who seem to be tied to specific objects, rather than locations. Research J. B. Rhine, the dean of American parapsychology, also collected stories of objects that seemed to collect and hold the "spiritual residue" of a person or situation. While such stories do exist, it must be said that they are rare in the realm of ghostlore.

Rarer still are tales of spirits who seem to attach themselves, not to a location or even object, but to a specific family, appearing in turn to not one but several generations. Such is the case of the "banshee" whose name has been whispered with trepidation and horror for centuries in the British Isles.

The origin of the banshee legend lies clouded in the mist of antiquity. Clearly, the most direct mention we have of her comes from ancient Celtic and Scottish mythology. In Scotland, the banshee is seen as a deathlike hag, with dark eyes set deep in a skull-like face. She is most often encountered at twilight along a stream, washing the bloodstained death clothes of those about to die.

In Ireland, her persona is said to be a bit more eye-catching but no less sinister. Rosemary Guiley, in the *Encyclopedia of Ghosts and Spirits*, defines a banshee as:

> A female death omen spirit of Ireland and Scotland that attaches itself to families…and manifests itself to herald an approaching death of a member of the family. To warn a family of a coming death, the banshee is heard most commonly singing or crying. When seen, she is said to be beautiful, with long streaming hair, often wearing all white or red. She is nearly always seen weeping, the sound of her crying so mournful it is unmistakably the sound of doom.

She is further described in Irish folklore as having long red or blonde hair and a beautiful face that is described as warped into a countenance of heartbreaking sorrow or soul rending grief. Whatever her appearance, it is the sound of her wailing that has sealed her fame, or infamy, in folklore. Throughout the centuries, many an Irish family has huddled close to their peat fire on a dark night, fear clutching their hearts at the mysterious sound of a woman wailing somewhere in the night. For such a family, the message of the banshee was clear: someone close was to die that night.

It should be noted that there are at least two facets of the banshee legend that make her doubly unique. One is that the banshee is never said to appear except to announce an impending death. Even then she is said to never appear to the one destined to die, instead making her presence known to the family of the doomed person. The second aspect that makes her unique in ghostlore is the fact that, (as has been noted), unlike most of the phantoms, the banshee attaches herself to families, following them for several generations, regardless of their proximity to their native land.

For the record, it should be stated that Lynne Hanley* knows little if anything about something as obscure as the lore of the banshee. Mrs. Hanley is not an expert on folklore or ghosts or anything of the kind. She is not a dabbler in the supernatural and candidly admits never having read a ghost story in her life. Rather, she is a retired insurance executive, currently living in Batesville, Indiana, in the southeast corner of the state.

At first glance, Lynne Hanley seems to be the last person one would expect to be reporting a ghost story. Now in her early sixties, she is still the picture of the efficient, thoroughly no-nonsense professional that she was for forty years of her life. Retirement has not dulled her spirit or energy for life. She is, as she admits, "someone who centers herself on the here and now," and portrays a vitality and level-headed outlook on life that belies any experience with the supernatural.

"I grew up in Metamora," Lynne states, "and moved to Indianapolis after I graduated from college in 1959. I ran the Midwest office for one of the big insurance carriers there for about twenty-five years. About five years ago, when the company was bought out and I was offered a chance for early retirement, I snapped at the opportunity. By then our kids had moved away from home, so my husband and I moved lock, stock and barrel back to southeastern Indiana where I grew up. I love it here and we have enjoyed our new home."

If this were the "typical" ghost story, one might next expect an account of how the new home to which Mrs. Hanley moved was inhabited by an unquiet specter and of the unearthly events that occurred in there. Such a classic tale would no doubt be replete with tales of ghostly voices emanating from empty hallways and unearthly shadows seen creeping up the stairs.

However, though Mrs. Hanley may not be aware of it, hers is anything but a typical ghost story. This is because the ghostly presence she has encountered not once but several times in the last sixty years of her life is not a run-of-the-mill specter. Indeed, as she tells the tale, hers is a phantom that is not linked to geography, but instead has been attached to her family lineage for many generations. Though she seems unaware of the term to be employed, according to the story she tells, it seems that her family has been the not-so-proud possessors of a form of a banshee spirit.

Interestingly, though the classic banshee legend attaches the ghost to strictly old Irish families, Mrs. Hanley is of proud Italian ancestry. "My maiden name is Lorento," she says, "and we were third generation Italians. My grandmother, my father's mother, had grown up in a small town in Sicily and we were raised on all the old traditions and especially all that great Italian food. Some of my best memories as a child were going to my grandmother's house every Sunday after church and sitting around the table with my cousins and aunts and uncles getting overfed on stuffed peppers and spaghetti. It was a great time and after dinner my grandma would start to talk about her family in Italy and all the times she had growing up in her village. I thought at the time that we knew everything there was to know about our family after those talks, but now I realize that the one part of our family heritage my grandma left out was *her*."

The "her" to which Mrs. Hanley refers is a strange specter she and her family have encountered throughout the years. It is a family tradition unspoken of in polite gatherings, lurking in the deepest and darkest part of their collective family identity.

"My first encounter with our ghost came when I was about sixteen and at the time I did not think anything about it," she now recalls. "My grandfather, who was about seventy at the time, was in one of the local hospitals dying of emphysema and, of course, the whole family was upset. My world was particularly rocked because this was the first person close to me to be facing death."

"Grandpa had been sick for some time and his weight had dropped from probably 220 pounds to maybe 150. Every week, my family and I had to traipse up to the hospital to see him and I have to honestly say that I dreaded it. Don't get me wrong—I loved my grandpa dearly, but I hated seeing him get sicker and sicker and to see him thinner each time I saw him. Still, we were a tight family and so as his death got closer, we would come more and more often."

Then came the night that the family had long feared and yet expected. "I remember I was home studying for a test the next day in school when the phone rang," Lynne remembers. "My dad answered the phone in the living room and there was a short conversation. Then he hung up and came into the kitchen, where my siblings and I were studying and told us to grab our coats because we were going to the hospital. There was something in his face that made me think things were pretty bad."

In the brief car ride to the hospital, Lynne's father explained that his sister had called and said that their father had taken a turn for the worse. As he was not expected to last the night, all the family was being called in. Gently and lovingly her father explained that death was imminent and tried to prepare his children for that eventuality. However, as events would turn out, nothing could prepare Lynne for one small, seemingly insignificant event that would meet her at the hospital.

"The whole family gathered at the hospital that night—all my aunts and uncles and cousins. We filled the whole room and we just sat there for maybe an hour watching my grandfather painfully gasping for breath. It was unpleasant to say the least. Finally, one of the nurses came in and kindly said that it was against policy to have twenty people in one room. She suggested that we move into a waiting room down the hall and take turns coming in to sit with grandpa. After watching him suffer for an hour I think at least we kids were only too happy to vacate the room and we moved down the hall to a spacious waiting room with a TV."

Throughout that long night, the family kept watch by turns at the bedside of the aged man. "Every so often, my dad or aunt would come back to the waiting room with some of our cousins who had been in to see him and another three or four of us would go in for a while. It was a sad time but as I look back it, it was also a close family time as well," Lynn says.

Finally, at about 2:00 A.M., Lynne remembers that her aunt came to her and gently whispered that her grandfather was close to death and that if she wished to pay her last respects, she should come to the room immediately. "I started to cry," Lynne remembers, "and as silly as it sounds, I did not want to see my grandfather looking like a mess so I told my Aunt Tina to go ahead into the room and that I would be there after I went to the bathroom. I was in the bathroom no more than a minute fixing myself up and then I walked down the empty hallway toward my grandfather's room."

As she slowly made her way toward the room, however, Lynne saw something that did not seem significant at the time, yet would later come to have eerie and mysterious meaning for her.

"As I walked toward the room, I saw a woman standing at the end of the hallway outside my grandfather's room. At first, I thought that it was a nurse but as I got closer I could see that she was dressed funny. She had on a long green gown—not a hospital gown but an ornate, old-fashioned formal dress with pleats going down the front. I did not get a good look at her because it was dark and my mind was on my grandpa but I do remember that she had long hair and as I got closer, I thought that she might be crying. It seemed odd but my mind was elsewhere, so I glanced at her for just a second and then went into the room."

There she found her grandfather barely clinging to life, his breath now coming in short gasps. "I remember that my father was there holding Grandpa's hand and my grandmother was in the corner crying. Dad said they had called in a priest for the last rites but they were not sure he would make it in time. I stood there, a sixteen-year-old kid not knowing what to say or do, just listing to the sound of my grandfather's labored breathing and my grandmother's soft crying."

As the minutes passed, however, Lynne became aware of an odd fact. "I realized that at least some of the crying I was hearing wasn't coming from the room, but from just outside in the hall. At first, I wondered if one of my cousins was waiting to come in, but then I thought of that strange woman and I wondered if she was losing someone she loved too."

However, this thought was soon forgotten as the local priest entered the room and began to administer the last rites to the dying man. Within half an hour, Lynne's grandfather had passed on and all thoughts of the mysterious woman were pushed from Lynne's mind as her family prepared for the funeral and wake.

"I did not think anything about that woman till after the funeral when we all went over to Grandma's house for an old fashioned Italian wake," Lynne recalls. "All of the family and friends where there. It was like a huge party, but that was the way we did things. After the dinner, I was sitting in the living room with a bunch of my cousins just talking when one of my cousins said, 'Did any of you see that weird woman standing in the hallway the night that grandpa died?' My ears perked up at that and I said, 'YES! That strange lady in the long gown!' "

At this, several of the other young people in the room denied having seen such a woman and began to excitedly quiz the pair about what they had seen. Interestingly, Lynne's cousin's description of the woman corresponded nearly exactly with her own but added the fact that as he had left the room that night, he had heard her softly moaning in the corner as if (in his words), "her heart was breaking."

"All of us kids were really curious about this woman and we talked about it for a few minutes. During the conversation, I happened to glance to the corner of the room where my Uncle Vince was sitting. He was staring at us with the strangest look on his face. After a minute, I turned to him and said, 'Uncle Vince, did you see that lady that night at the hospital?' He just looked down for a minute and then said, 'No, there was no lady at the hospital. It was probably just some nurse.' I started to tell him it wasn't any nurse we had seen but he just got up and walked into the kitchen without saying another word."

After that day, the subject of the strange woman in the long gown was dropped and Lynne says she never thought of it again for several years. It might have remained submerged in her subconscious memories, never to be remembered again, except for the fact that fate seemed to deem that she meet this strange woman again.

"The next part of the story seems incredible, even to me," Lynne says. "It happened about five years later when I was a junior at Purdue and I got a phone call that my Aunt Theresa was dying of cancer. She had been fighting it for a couple of years but just that month, her condition had deteriorated rapidly. My dad called me at school and said that the doctors had given her only a week at most to live and at her request, they had taken her home. It seems she wanted to die in her own bed."

"My dad told me that I needed to come home so I talked to my professors the next day and then drove home that night. I got there about eight o'clock and my parents were already over at Aunt Theresa's house, so I just dropped off my stuff and went over. Her house was out in the country, down a dark road, but I when I pulled in the driveway, I saw that all the outside lights were on, illuminating the drive and yard. I can still picture it—it was a windy spring night and the branches of the trees were tossing back and forth in the breeze."

As Lynne walked toward the house, the door was opened by her mother, who welcomed her and brought her to the living room. There she found two of her brothers and one of her sisters waiting. "We talked for a few moments," Mrs. Hanley relates, "and then Dad came down and told me that I should go up to see Aunt Theresa—he said that he had told her I was coming and she was asking for me."

Leaving her family in the living room, Lynne went upstairs to the hallway that led to her aunt's room. "I went into Aunt Theresa's room and sat by her bed for a few minutes. She was really weak but her mind was clear and she was glad to see me. She was actually in good spirits and we laughed a little and remembered some of the good times we had shared. It was a sad but touching visit, and then after about twenty minutes, she seemed to be getting weaker so I told her she should rest. Then I left the room and quietly shut the door and started to walk back down the hall to the stairs."

However, about halfway down the hall, Lynne's progress was arrested by a sight that nearly stopped her heart.

"I will never forget it," she says. "The memory still raises bumps on the back of my hand. Halfway down that hall, I passed a window looking out onto the front yard. As I glanced out the window I saw a figure standing in the yard looking up at the house. She was clearly illuminated by the yard lights as she stood there underneath one of those wind blown trees. *I know how crazy this sounds, but it was the same woman I had seen in the hospital the night my grandfather died.*"

Her heart rising in her chest, Lynne stood at the window, transfixed by the sight before her. "She was unmistakable," she says, emotion creeping into her voice. "She wore the same long gown and in my shock, I still realized that even though the wind was whipping the trees around her, her hair wasn't moving. It was like a picture, except for what happened next. As I stood there, she raised her face to look directly at the window where I stood. It was like our eyes locked and I think that for a moment my heart stopped. The lights from the house shone on her, but she also seemed to be bathed in a glow all her own. Her hair was wild and unkempt but it is her face that I remember most—it was beautiful in its way, yet she had an expression of extreme sorrow. It was the saddest face that I had ever seen. I was not close enough to be sure but I think that her mouth was moving like she was saying something I could not hear and I somehow knew she was crying."

As Lynne describes her feelings in that moment, she says that she felt an odd mixture of shock and disbelief, mixed in with a healthy dose of fear, yet underneath it all lay an overwhelming sense of grief. "When the woman looked up at me standing by the window, I felt the most profound sense of sadness I have ever felt. It just enveloped me and I think somehow, that the feeling was related to her. I have no idea how long I stood there," she now remembers, "feeling this flood of astonishment and fear. I felt like I literally could not move, but I must have blinked or looked away for a second, because when I looked back she was just gone. It was that quick."

"Oddly, the shock of her vanishing was almost as bad as the jolt of seeing her," Lynne recalls, "and I let out a scream that brought my mother and father running up from downstairs. I think I kind of collapsed into my father's arms and they helped me downstairs. I was crying and they kept asking me what had happened. Finally, I blurted out what I had seen and my brother immediately went outside to see if anyone was there, but my dad did not budge an inch. He sat there for a long time and then said, 'It has been a long day for you. I'll get your brother to drive you home so that you can get some rest.' I asked him point blank if he believed me and my dad, who was a very direct man, just said, 'I'm not sure what to believe but I know you're upset, so I think you should go home.' So that is what I did."

Sadly, Lynne's Aunt Theresa died a week later and the subject of the strange woman was never discussed further with her family. Lynne recalls that each time she attempted to bring up the incident, her father abruptly changed the subject and after a short time she gave up, deciding that the entire event must have been some sort of a hallucination. Finally, after her aunt's funeral, she returned to her studies at Purdue, still unsettled by the event.

"I tried not to think about the whole thing. It all seemed so incredible I actually thought I might be going nuts. But then, a couple of summers later, something happened that changed all that," Lynne says.

"It was the summer after I had graduated in 1959 and I was fresh with a degree in business and no job in sight," Lynne continues. "I had applications in all over but I had not gotten a solid offer yet, so I was just sort of bumming around home when my aunt, who ran a bookstore in Columbus, offered me a job helping out for the summer. It was low wage but it was a paycheck and besides, I would get to work with my cousin Lucy, who was about two years younger than I. We had grown up together and were really close."

During the long summer afternoons, the two girls would mind the store. In the time when business was lapse, the pair would spend hours talking and laughing in the easy familiarity of young women who share a common family bond. It was on one such afternoon that Lucy shared a story with her cousin that would shake Lynne to the core.

"It was probably mid-July," Lynne says, "and I had been working there for about a month. As I remember it, Lucy had been gone from the store all morning and by the time she got there in the afternoon we had just gotten a big shipment in. So, since business was slow, we both went into the back room and unpacked the boxes, listening for the door chime to let us know if a customer came in.

"We were both sitting in the back room. I remember it was really hot because the back was not air conditioned, and we started talking about the usual stuff—who we were going out with that weekend, what new clothes we had bought—all the standard stuff. Suddenly Lucy brightened up and said, 'I just remembered, Lynne—the weirdest thing happened to me last night!' "

As Lynne listened, her cousin told her that the previous evening she had driven to nearby North Vernon to meet some college friends for a movie and then had gone with them to a restaurant for a late night snack before heading home.

"Lucy told me that the evening had been an enjoyable one, until she got into the car to head home," Lynne recalls. "As she related it to me, she got into the car, started it, and started backing up when suddenly, glancing into the rearview mirror, she saw a woman standing directly behind her car. She could see her illuminated in the brake lights. She slammed on the brakes, thinking that the woman was just walking through the parking lot to her car, but instead of moving on, the woman just stood there staring at her. She said it gave her the creeps. Lucy said she finally decided that the woman might want to say something, so she rolled down her window and leaned out, but suddenly the woman was gone. She swore she was gone in just the matter of a second.

"When Lucy told me her story, I did not think much of it, but then she added one afterthought that made me sit up and take notice. After she had told me the story she said, 'She had the strangest expression on her face as she stood there staring at me, but what was really strange was the clothes this lady was wearing. It was a long formal green gown that was pleated down the front and she had long, wild-looking hair.' When she said that, it brought back everything that I had seen and I got all excited and told her about seeing the strange woman at the hospital and at my aunt's house."

"It sounded impossible, but we both wondered if it could possibly be the same woman. We jokingly wondered if she was some crazy aunt that the family had disowned and so now she was stalking us. Then my cousin said, 'Maybe she's a ghost!' She thought that was funny, but having seen this lady twice, I have to say I did not laugh."

The girls resolved to talk to Lucy's aunt about the woman when she came in that afternoon, to see if anyone else in the family had ever seen her. When the woman arrived, the two girls regaled her with their tales and asked her if she had ever seen a woman like that. "My aunt seemed amused and genuinely puzzled," Lynne remembers. "She said that she had never seen anyone fitting that description and she assured us that there was no secret relative running around. Then, just as she turned to go, she said, 'By the way, girls, speaking of our family, I got a phone call this morning that my great aunt, your grandpa's aunt, died last night in Pittsburgh.' " A seemingly insignificant and unrelated comment, yet one that would later tie together events for Lynne.

Despite her aunt's assurances, Lynne's curiosity and sense of intrigue over the phantom woman were not quelled. She also says that she could not escape the impression that this woman's appearances were somehow connected with her family in some way. Unsure of what to do, Lynne thought of going to her father once more, but his uncharacteristically unsympathetic response to her questions previously made her wary of approaching him again.

"I guess I brooded over it most of that summer," Lynne remembers, "and then toward August, I was offered a job in Indianapolis. I was delighted to get a good job but I was also glad that this would put me closer to my grandmother. By that point, she was living with my Aunt Margaret just outside the city. I had not seen too much of her since she had moved there a few years before and I wanted to see her again. She was probably in her early nineties by then and mostly bed-ridden, but her mind was still sharp as a tack. She spoke broken English at best but she could talk for hours."

Lynne relates that in the weeks and months after she moved to Indianapolis, she took pleasure in frequently visiting her grandmother in her aunt's home and the pair would chat about everything from Lynne's new life to the old woman's childhood in Sicily. Frequently, their talks led them to discussions of their family and its history.

"As we continued to talk, the subject of this strange woman came to my mind again and again, but I could not summon up the courage to mention to her what I had seen," Lynne says. "But then, one evening I finally got up the nerve. It was a Friday afternoon after work and I stopped by, as usual, to spend time with Grandma. My aunt made us all dinner and I ate with Grandma in her room. She started talking that night about Grandpa and all their years together. Then she started talking about his final illness in the hospital and suddenly I just interrupted her and said. 'Grandma, I saw something…on the night grandpa died…' and then I just blurted out the whole story.

"I told her about the woman I saw in the hall that night and about seeing the same woman at Aunt Theresa's house and about how I thought my cousin Lucy had seen the same woman in the parking lot the night that another family member had died. Once I started talking it just all came out. I don't know what I expected Grandma to say. I guess I should have expected her to tell me I was crazy. But Grandma just laid back against her pillow and listened and when I was done I looked over and saw tears running down her cheeks."

"I looked at Grandma and did not know what to say," Lynne continues. "I was afraid that I had upset her with all this death talk but I will never forget what happened next. She reached out and took my hand and murmured something in Italian. I asked her what she had said and she kind of caught her herself, like she was only then remembering I did not speak Italian, and she said in her thick accent '*It means woman of death.*' "

"In her halting, broken English she then told me that when she married my grandfather, he had told her that she would always know when he was going to die because the woman of death would come for him, just as she had for all of his family. He told her that for centuries, the story had been handed down in his family that any time a member of the family was about to die, the woman of death would always be seen, or at least heard crying. He said that my grandma would probably never see her because she was not a member of the family by blood but that someone always saw her when a death approached."

"I sat there listening to this terrible story and all those feelings of shock and disbelief came back to me. Of course it was natural for my grandmother to believe in all that stuff because she was…an Old World Sicilian after all. But here I was, a modern career girl, and it went against everything that I believed. Up to that point I would have dismissed what Grandma said entirely but for one thing. *I had seen her myself* and so had at least two of my cousins that I knew of. I asked Grandma if anyone else in the family had ever seen her, and she nodded her head and told me that my Aunt Theresa had seen her and so had my Uncle Vince once, years ago, when he was a child. For me, that explained his reaction when he heard my cousin and me talking about the woman that afternoon in Grandma's living room."

"My head was really whirling from all of this and I think that I finally said to Grandma something like, 'So this is like a family curse, right?' but my grandma squeezed my hand and said, 'No! She is not a curse. She is a blessing.' When I looked surprised she explained, 'To you, the young, death is an enemy. To the old, like me, death is a welcome friend. This lady, she does not cause death but I think she comes to bring the comfort of death to the ones who are ready for it. She cries when we see her, but I do not think she cries for the one going to heaven. I think she cries for the ones who see her—the living ones. I am not blood family, so she will not come for me, but one day, when you're old like me, maybe she will come for you to take you to God. Then you will understand.' "

True to her words, when Lynne's grandmother died several years later, the woman of death did not make an appearance. However, the words of the old woman remained with her and have been a comfort ever since. Over time, Lynne has shared the "family secret" with all of her brothers and sister and several of her cousins. Most seem willing to write the story off as ancient family folklore, yet the tale has a profound effect on Lynne's view of life and of death. It is a view that has helped her through the death of both of her parents, as well as one brother and a nephew.

It should be noted that with the death of her father and brother, no one reported seeing the phantom woman—although in at least one instance, a family member reported the sound of crying coming from an empty hallway a few days before the passing of their loved one. However, it was the tragic death of her young nephew that provided Lynne with the impression that perhaps the woman has not abandoned her familial post.

"My nephew, Jimmy, was born in 1973 with severe birth defects,"

Lynne says. "They did not expect him to live the first few days of life but he pulled through, although he was mentally and physically handicapped and his health was precarious at best. His twelve years of life were one round of hospitalization after another, and eventually my sister and her husband moved out east to be near a hospital that specialized in treating kids like Jimmy."

By the time of the boy's twelfth birthday, his health had deteriorated to the point that all concerned knew his life expectancy was short. "We, of course, were still in Indianapolis and my kids were still in school. We could not make it out to New York when Jimmy got bad," Lynne says. "However, I was in daily phone contact with my sister Connie. In September, Jimmy was put in the hospital one final time and by the middle of the month, he passed away. There was no funeral right away since his parents wanted to bring his ashes back home for a memorial service around Christmas time. So I just stayed at home and wrote letters and made phone calls to Connie. All things considered, she was doing pretty well."

Then, in the first week of November, Lynne received a letter from her sister that she has saved ever since. It was a general letter of thanks and appreciation for the family support she had received and an update on her family's activities since the death of their oldest son. At the conclusion of the letter, however, her sister wrote one paragraph relating to her youngest son, John, which riveted Lynne's attention.

"In all the commotion, I think I forgot to tell you one story that you might find interesting. About three days before Jimmy passed, I got back from the hospital about midnight and went right to sleep. About 1:00 A.M., the door to our room opened and John came in and asked to come to bed with us. At ten he is a little old for that bit, but I knew we were all upset about Jimmy so I rolled over and let him in. He told me that he had had a dream and I asked him what it was. He said a weird woman had come into his room and stood next to his bed crying. He said she had on a big dress like they wore in the movies. I was so tired that I did not think about it but since then, I remembered the stories that you used to tell about our family ghost. John has never heard the stories but he now claims that it was not a dream at all but was real and so maybe your spook is still at work. I don't know what to think."

The grieving mother may be forgiven her uncertainty, but in her mind, Lynne Hanley believes that she understands. She believes that it was indeed the family spirit coming to announce the death of a loved one as she has for untold generations. Moreover, just as her grandmother predicted, Lynne no longer sees the woman as a grim, ominous creature, but instead, as a strange sort of friend. "I know that it sounds weird," she says with a sigh, "but I hope that when it is my time to go that the lady comes for me too, just as she did for my grandpa and aunt. It is somehow reassuring to think that she is there, waiting till the time I am ready to go to God."

It should be noted that Lynne Hanley knows nothing of the legend of the banshee. She is not concerned with the world of the supernatural nor the realm of ghostlore. However, this pragmatic, vital lady sees herself as a woman whose family is the recipient of an extraordinary curse, or, in her view, blessing—an otherworldly family visitor who appears at that moment when one life is ready to end and a better life is ready to begin. She provides a sense of continuity for her family and a sense of peace as Lynne Hanley approaches her twilight years. Hers is a strange and chilling tale, even by the standards of "conventional" ghost stories. Whether a harbinger of death or the bearer of eternal peace, she is truly an extraordinary part of Indiana ghostlore.

10
WHEN DEATH CAME TO THE BIG TOP
Hammond, Indiana[10]

"Eleven fifty-five. Almost midnight. Enough time for one more story. One more story before 12...just to keep us warm..."

Mr. Machen , "The Fog"

The old adage states that it is always darkest before the dawn. As conductor J. W. Johnson peered out of his locomotive in the moments preceding dawn on the morning of June 22, 1918, the darkness around him seemed as black as pitch. Behind him, the line of twenty-five cars his engine was pulling, making up the second section of the famed Hagenbeck-Wallace Circus train, was quickly swallowed up in the darkness.

The train had been slowing for almost a half mile. Now, with the sharp bark of escaping steam, it came to a complete stop. Behind him, the engineer knew that crewmen were quickly scrambling down from the caboose and into the early morning chill to look for the faulty gearbox (or hotbox as it was known) that had been reported a mile or so back as the train crossed Colfax Street. For at least the next few minutes, the circus train would sit dead on the tracks until the problem could be corrected, but Johnson was not concerned. He knew that signal #2581 had gone red a mile behind him, warning any train coming in behind to stop. He also knew that railroad law prohibited any train from traveling more than twenty-five miles per hour over this section of track, giving an engineer ample time to slow his train after seeing the signal. As the resonant thrum of the engine at rest filled the air around him, Johnson turned back to monitor the gauges glowing in the darkness of his cab.

If the engineer had glanced at his watch, he would have seen that it was 3:56 A.M. For him this was just another stop along a journey that was almost complete. He knew that in a few moments, as dawn began to paint the eastern sky behind him, the repairs would be finished and the train would be on its way. He also knew that in a matter of less than an hour, as his 225 passengers disembarked and began the laborious process of setting up the circus for that day's performance, his day would end.

What he did not know at that moment was that in the cars behind him, eighty-six people were living the last thirty-eight seconds of their lives. Dawn would never come for them on that fateful morning, as death itself came hurdling headlong down the tracks behind them.

The Hagenbeck-Wallace Circus train disaster would come to be known as one of the worst train disasters in the twentieth century. Curiously, while the accident made national news at the time, most Hoosiers living in northwest Indiana today have little or no knowledge of its existence. It is through the efforts of the Hammond Historical Society, and in particular the late Walter A. Reeder, Jr., that the history of this disaster has been preserved. Indeed, Mr. Reeder, an avid historian and exhaustive researcher, spent many years of his life investigating the history of the disaster and collecting interviews with those survivors still alive at the time. In 1972, his exacting research culminated in his writing the fascinating book, *No Performances Today,* an exhaustive chronicle of that fateful night. It is from this source that nearly all understanding of those events can be drawn.

The Hagenbeck-Wallace Circus had become an Indiana institution years before that dreadful night. Its roots began when Ben Wallace returned to his home in Peru, Indiana, after service in the Union army in the Civil War. While in the army, Wallace served in the cavalry, feeding and caring for horses. Upon his return, Wallace set himself up in the livery business, and in particular with the business of buying and selling horses. Such was his skill in equine training that he soon began to put on shows for the local populace and in 1886, the "Great Wallace Show" hit the rails for the first time. In the next several decades, Wallace began to acquire other shows and eventually circuses. These were transported by rail across the Midwest, to the delight of small town audiences near and far.

It should be noted that rail travel at the time was not without its risks. An ominous portent of things to come for the Hagenbeck-Wallace Circus occurred on August 7, 1903, when the Wallace Circus was pulling into a train station in Durand, Michigan. The second section of the circus train came roaring into the railroad yards at a terrific rate of speed, ramming into the rear of the first section and killing twenty-six people.

Still, the Wallace Circus continued to grow over the next several years. In 1907 Wallace purchased the Hagenbeck Animal Circus of Europe, forming the Hagenbeck-Wallace Circus. Based on a two hundred-acre farm in Peru, Indiana, adjacent to a ninety-five-acre railway yard dedicated for its use, the Hagenbeck-Wallace Circus traveled across the nation, rising to the role of one of the leading traveling shows of its day. A few years later, Wallace retired from the business, selling out to the American Circus Corporation. Under their guidance, the show continued to tour and prosper. By 1918, the Hagenbeck-Wallace Circus could boast of a show featuring "60 aerialists, 60 acrobats, 60 riders and 50 clowns." All told, the circus consisted of twenty-two tents, a thousand employees, and a payroll of $7,500 per day.

During the years preceding the first world war, as the Hagenbeck-Wallace Show toured the nation, the growing steel city of Hammond became on of their favorite places for a show. They appeared successfully in that city in 1907, 1910, 1912, and 1914. Even when wartime travel restrictions curtailed their show schedule, the circus kept Hammond as one of their featured locations.

On the night of June 21, 1918, the Hagenbeck-Wallace Circus was finishing up two shows in Michigan City, Indiana. The next day they were scheduled to appear in Hammond for one show before taking a well-deserved day off on Sunday. At about 9:00 P.M., the first section of the circus, consisting of all the animals and about half of the performers, left the Michigan City station bound for Hammond. By 2:00 A.M., the tents had been torn down and the second section of the circus prepared to depart. On the station platform that early morning, unknowing participants in a fateful drama were making fateful decisions.

Joe Coyle, a clown with the circus, begged Mr. Gollmer, the general manager, to allow his wife to travel with him on the train to Hammond, against official circus policy. Reluctantly, Gollmer agreed. Mayme Ward, an aerialist, nearly missed the train after visiting with family in the city. However, she did reach the train and went into her sleeping compartment for what she assumed would be a good night's rest. Meanwhile, nationally known trick rider Ken Maynard was about to take the second section of the train but delayed his departure in order to spend a few more precious hours with a young lady he had met in Michigan City. For all of these performers and many more, life would never be the same after that night.

When conductor J. W. Johnson fired the engine of his locomotive, pulling the second section of the circus train out of the Michigan City depot, his orders were simple and direct. They called for his train to go via the Michigan City tracks to Ivanhoe, a small station between Gary and Hammond, then switch onto the Michigan Central Tracks and thus into Hammond. Once in Hammond, he would direct the locomotive to a side rail that would take them to the lot where the circus would play near 150th and Calumet.

The first hour of the trip was uneventful as the steam locomotive chugged its way through the silent Indiana landscape, its mournful whistle echoing out into the night air as they neared each road crossing. However, just as the train passed Colfax Street, the fireman behind Johnson relayed the message that the brakeman in the caboose had seen a hotbox on one of the cars. No doubt Johnson was more annoyed than alarmed by the report.

In those days, a hotbox was a common problem on railway cars. The box itself was a metal container covering each side of each axle on the freight cars. Since these axles depended on grease for lubrication and since the grease deteriorated with use, the hot box was designed to begin to glow when the axle grew hot, alerting train personnel that a problem existed. While certainly serious enough to stop the train, in reality it was a routine problem, remedied by simply removing the box and replacing the grease. Usually, this process was a matter of no more than fifteen minutes.

Somewhat reluctantly, Johnson began to slow his train to a stop. By the time it ground to a halt, the main section of the train had turned off onto the Michigan Central tracks with only the last five cars still resting on the main line. Still, this hardly represented a danger, since the signals behind would warn any oncoming train of their presence. Had the fates been kinder that night, this would have been nothing more than a routine stop on a routine journey.

However, on this night, the fates were anything but kind. On this night death was riding the rails toward the circus train. Coming in fast and hard behind the Hagenbeck-Wallace train, there was another train. Engine 8545 was pulling an empty troop train on its way to Chicago to pick up a load of soldiers destined for the front lines of France. It was yet another nameless train on yet another nameless trip. However, on this night, something was terribly wrong. For as engine 8545 and the fourteen cars it was pulling steamed through the night, it seemed to be traveling abnormally fast.

The fireman in the coal car noted that the steam coming from the smoke stack did not sound as it should—instead of the gentle series of puffs it normally emitted, the sound was a constant harsh shrill. From years of experience on the railroad, the fireman knew what this meant. The engine was running at full throttle, in violation of speed ordinance on that section of the rail. As he later testified, the fireman was further alarmed when he saw, as they approached the Ivanhoe station, that the engineer, Alonzo Sargent, was ignoring all warning lights. As he would remark years later, "I saw him pass those lights and wondered what he was about—I wondered what in the world he was doing."

Had the fireman in question been able to glimpse into the cab of the engine, he would have readily understood—for in the gentle glow of the control lights he would have seen conductor Alonzo Sargent slumped over, fast asleep as his train headed toward disaster.

As the troop train hurdled headlong past the Colfax Street crossing, the brakeman on the circus train had just climbed out of his caboose and begun trudging toward the hotbox glowing beneath the car ahead. Suddenly, his attention was riveted to a sound coming from behind—a steam engine thundering toward them at full speed. In a moment, the lights of the train appeared behind, heading directly to-

Photo courtesy of the Walter A. Reeder, Jr. Family

Original photos taken the morning of June 22, 1918, of the crash of the Hagenbeck-Wallace circus train, just outside of Hammond, Indiana.

ward him and his train. Thinking quickly, he ran back to his caboose and grabbed a set of fusees, or small safety flares, kept there for emergencies. Lighting one, he waved it wildly in the air, seeking to warn the oncoming train. As the engine did not seem to slow, the brakeman lit a second flare and then a third but the engine came on heedlessly. Finally, as the train drew to within a few yards of the stopped circus train, the valiant brakeman threw his lit flare directly at the cab of the oncoming locomotive in a last, futile attempt at alerting the engineer. As the fusee exploded against the cab in a shower of sparks, the troop train smashed into the caboose with an explosive force.

At 3:57 A.M., Engine 8445 hit the rear section of the Hagenbeck-Wallace Circus train at approximately thirty-five miles per hour. Though the speed may not seem excessive by today's standards, the force of the collision sent the engine careening at least four hundred feet through the caboose and last five sleeping cars of the train before stopping crossways on the tracks. As neighbor Mrs. Bert Moser described the sound for the *Chicago Tribune* the next day, "There was a crash, a roar and a long drawn out sound, as if a million bricks were crashing onto a tin roof. Then absolute silence."

In that deathly silence, a terrible catastrophe became truly horrific. As the engine tore through the rear of the Hagenbeck-Wallace Circus train, it plowed up the last five sleeping cars before it, stacking them up one on top of another into a nearly unrecognizable mass. No doubt many of the hapless souls in those cars died instantly. Still many more lay injured or buried in the rubble. This, however was not to be the worst of the wreck. Many more would have lived to see the morning light that was just moments away except for two facts.

The first was that the sleeping cars used by the Hagenbeck-Wallace Circus Train were of Civil War vintage design and were constructed completely of wood. The second fact to seal the fate of those alive beneath the wreckage was that those cars had been lit solely by gasoline-fueled lamps.

In the moments after Engine 8485 had ground to a stop, first a spark and a small plume of flame shot from within the depths of the wreckage. Within moments, the night sky of northern Indiana was lit by bright flame as the wreck turned into a fiery inferno. Most of those trapped and injured in the wreckage never stood a chance. As Warren Reeder records the scene in *No Performances Today:*

> One of the ghastly sights following the wreck was the sight of two men, not identified, who were caught between two of the coaches, jammed together with mattresses about them. The mattresses caught fire and the terrible countenances of the doomed men were framed in the flames like martyrs burning at the stake. Their screams sounded above the moans and groans of all others about them. They were cremated.

Many of the eighty-six who were to die that night met a similar fate, incinerated beyond recognition. Indeed, records from the time reflect that nearly half of the remains later recovered could not be identified.

Police and firemen, called by those living in the vicinity of the wreck, arrived within a short time, but the first real rescue train did not arrive till almost an hour after the wreck. When rescuers did arrive, a grotesque sight met their eyes. By then the light of the new day revealed a tangled mass of wreckage still burning brightly. The injured and dying were lying about the tracks, some screaming and pleading for help. A few waved the rescuers away, begging only to be allowed to die. Some of the uninjured circus personnel were still seeking to enter the wreckage to pull out more survivors as they had been doing since the accident, but firemen and ambulance workers could quickly tell that there could be none left alive in the flames and debris.

Others wandered aimlessly amid the dead and dying, unable to fathom the sight before them. Among them was Alonzo Sargent, conductor of the troop train. As he stood and stared in disbelief at the carnage before him, he was approached by the crewman who had served as his fireman on the engine. As the fireman later testified, "I asked him what had happened and he stared at me for a moment and then said, 'I was dozing—otherwise asleep.' "

Another visitor to the site that early morning was Gary Mayor William Hodges. As he later described the scene to reporters,

> It was one of the worst wrecks I have ever witnessed. The injured were lying in many different places. Bodies of the dead were strewn along the tracks. The cars were in flames. We saw several bodies in the ruins. Someone said that there were twenty-five bodies in the remains of one car. Most of these were women.

One man found the body of his wife in the weeds. He tried to comfort her but when he learned that she had been killed, his consciousness seemed to collapse. Rescuers shortly carried him to the relief train."

As more and more rescuers and onlookers arrived at the site, other gruesome discoveries were found. A number of severed fingers littered the rails. At least one charred head was found under the cow-catcher of the troop train. Most of the wreckage and nearly all the dead were found in a pile just to the front of where Engine 8485 had come to rest after doing its deadly work.

By noon, the fire was extinguished and the gruesome work of removing the last bodies and clearing the tracks could begin. The injured had been transported to five area hospitals, while at the circus lot in Hammond, a sense of numb disbelief prevailed. It was, as one circus worker later recalled, "as if someone had gutted the soul from our troop."

Still, amazingly, the old show business adage of "the show must go on" prevailed with the Hagenbeck-Wallace Circus. As word of the disaster spread, other circuses, most notably the Barnum Brothers Circus, sent offers of help. A new circus tent was procured and acts were "borrowed" from competing circuses. Against all odds, the Hagenbeck-Wallace Circus left Hammond two days later to fulfill its show commitments. Despite loosing nearly a quarter of its workforce to death and injury, the circus missed only two dates that season.

When the circus left Hammond that day, it left behind many of its members recuperating in area hospitals and many more in area morgues. Slowly, those bodies that could be identified were transported to their families for burial. However, many of the remains could not be identified and family could not be located for some.

On June 26, these were buried in a mass plot at Woodlawn Cemetery, just outside of Chicago, in a section known as "Showman's Rest." On that bright morning, over 1,500 people gathered on the green grass to listen as three clergymen read the funeral service. Before them lay a mass grave measuring thirty-five by twenty-five feet. In it lay fifty-six coffins. Of the fifty-six buried at Woodlawn, only fourteen could be identified. Curiously, even of these were some whose professions were known but whose names could not be ascertained, or whose identities were only partially known. Eventually, after the sod over the graves had been replaced, headstones were placed over these graves bearing such unique inscriptions as "Baldy" and "Four Horse Driver." Between these headstones were erected statues of three elephants walking, their trunks lowered in a sign of grief.

Interestingly, over the years a strange, unearthly. and ultimately unfounded story began to circulate in the area around Woodlawn cemetery about these mass graves. In the early 1970s, passersby began to report the sound of wild animals roaring from within the precincts of the cemetery grounds, particularly late at night. Rumors spread that a contingent of the circus animals had been killed in the train wreck and had been buried with their handlers in the mass grave. It was whispered that it was their ghosts that were being heard. In time, these tall tales began to be accepted as fact and the reports made their way into the media and eventually into the collective folklore of Chicago.

In reality, no animals of any kind had been boarded on the Hagenbeck-Wallace train that night, all of the livestock having come in later earlier on the first section. All of the remains interred in the mass grave at Woodlawn were of human origin. However, the mystery of the sounds emanating from the gravesite remained.

This part of the enigma was solved in the early 1980s when a local police officer who had several times heard the apparent "phantom" sounds himself investigated and found a simple answer. Standing at the mass grave one bright morning, the officer began to look around him and take careful note of his geographical location. Referring to a map, the officer easily saw the answer that had evaded so many for so long. Specifically, the map showed him that he was less than three quarters of a mile from Bookfield Zoo, where hundreds of exotic animals were housed. With this realization came the understanding that at times (particularly at night when nocturnal animals such as lions were active), the sounds of their roaring could be carried on the wind toward Woodlawn Cemetery which was just out of sight, but not out of earshot of the spot.

When news of this simple explanation was published, as it subsequently has been in two books on Chicago ghosts, (including Ursula Bielski's classic *Chicago Haunts*), no doubt fans of ghostlore were disappointed. However, this spurious ghost tale, although well known, is not the only supernatural tale told surrounding the Hagenbeck-Wallace Circus train tragedy. Just a few miles from Woodlawn Cemetery, across the Indiana border at the accident site, other bizarre tales have been told since that fateful night. These tales have not received the wide press coverage that had accompanied the spurious animal sounds coming from the Woodlawn mass grave. Instead, so macabre and unearthly are some of these stories that they have been whispered down through the decades in railway yards and across breakfast tables throughout Indiana. These are tales that have caused some to doubt their very sanity.

One person who has heard such tales is Oscar Cerentes, a retired railroad worker who lives in East Chicago. Oscar has been retired for fifteen years from the railroad, but for the preceding thirty-eight years his working life was spent as a switchmat a local railroad in northwest Indiana. As such, he had frequent opportunity to talk to many who had worked on the railroad and in time he would hear some unsettling stories.

"When I first started on the railroad, I had never heard of the circus train wreck, much less of any ghost stories associated with it," Oscar recalls. "But all that changed one night in the switching yard. I remember it was a January night—about twenty degrees below zero—and we were waiting for a train to come in. A couple of us were in the shanty trying to unfreeze our fingers by wrapping them around a cup of hot coffee. The wind was blowing hard and we were huddled in the center of the shack around a small heating stove.

"We were talking about the railroad," he continues, "and one of the old timers on the crew, a guy we called Stosh, mentioned that he had been an engineer for a long time before going back into the yard. That surprised me because once these guys got on the trains, they tended to stay there forever, so I asked him why he got kicked off. I kiddingly asked him if he was because of 'Rule G,' which is the law prohibiting engineers from drinking on the job.

"When I asked that question I remember that all of a sudden everyone just quit talking and they looked at me like I should learn to shut up, but the old guy I was talking to looked me right in the eye and said 'I quit because of something you would never believe in a million years.' I felt kind of funny for having asked an uncomfortable question of my elders, so I just told him I was sorry if I had offended him. He quickly let it pass and so we talked about something else. Still, my curiosity got the best of me and later, after the shift was over and we were cleaning up to go home, I asked another of the old timers named Hank what the problem was in the shanty with Stosh."

With a puff of his cigarette, Oscar recalls, "Hank took me over to the side and told me that everyone in that section of the railway knew that Stosh had asked to leave the trains because of something he had seen out by Ivanhoe station one night. He told me about the wreck of the circus train—that was the first time I had heard of it. Then he told me that the story was that one night about a year after Stosh had started working as an engineer, about 1938 that would have been, he drove his engine into the switching yard screaming something about a train wreck. He told the supervisor that he had passed a bad wreck just outside of Ivanhoe. He swore that he had seen cars crumpled up and flames everywhere. He even told the supervisor that it looked like an old steam locomotive had driven like hell through the middle of another train.

"Naturally, the supervisor told him that if there had been any kind of a wreck, he would have heard of it and that all the trains were running on schedule that night. According to the story, Stosh dragged him into the station and made him wire up and down the line asking about any wrecks, but everything was clear that night. After that the line supervisor smelled Stosh's breath thinking that he had been in his cups, but he was clean as a whistle. They even hauled old Stosh up in front of a railroad board of investigation, but he would not back off of his story—he stuck to what he said he had seen. He even asked to be taken off of the locomotive rather than back down on his story.

"When Hank finished telling me that story," Oscar now says, "I didn't know what to think, so I just shrugged it off and went home to tell my wife about it. Then I guess I just kind of forgot about the whole thing." However, this would not be the last time that Oscar would hear about the eerie goings on outside the Ivanhoe station. "About ten years later," Oscar remembers, "I was working the night shift and was sitting in the switching yard office about 4:00 A.M. when this engineer on an incoming westbound freight radioed in all frantic about some sort of an explosion at the line split. The supervisor radioed him back and asked for details and the guy said that as he was moving along westbound, he had seen a flash of bright light in the distance in front of him and had heard a muffled explosion.

"He had hit the brakes and slowed his engine down thinking that there had been a derailment ahead of him but when he got to the area where he had seen the flash of light, nothing was there. I remember the supervisor got this funny look on his face and asked the engineer exactly where he had seen the bright light. 'It seemed to come from the switch off from the main line, just east of Ivanhoe,' the guy came back. At that, the supervisor told the engineer to continue on his way and that nothing had happened along that track that night."

"As I sat there listening to all of this," Oscar recalls, "I did not make any connection to the old story about Stosh seeing the wreck on that stretch of rail. But when the supervisor got off the radio, I asked him if he wanted the boys and me to get an engine and go over to check out the switching. He just looked at me and said 'No Oscar, we have had those reports before out of that section. Trust me, nothing is there. In fact, I don't think that you should tell the other guys about this report. It did not happen.' "

It was only later when (against his supervisor's directive) Oscar shared the story with some of his fellow workers that he was reminded that it was on that stretch of rail at about 4:00 A.M. in 1918 when the Hagenbeck-Wallace Circus train had met its fate.

Many such quiet rumors seem to have been passed among the railroad workers in the area. While today many of those who claimed to have seen or heard things on that stretch of railroad have passed on, still some remember having heard the tales. Another person who re- members hearing of an incident is Peggy Parkinson*, a nurse who works in Hammond.

"When I was a little girl, my dad John worked for a long time as a brakeman on the railroad," Peggy remembers. "He worked long hours, but would come home with wonderful stories about riding in the loco- motive engine and what they had hauled that particular day. Looking back, they were pretty much everyday stuff for the railroad man, but for me as a little girl they were fascinating. Dad quit the railroad in the sixties and went to work in the mill, but still he loved to tell those stories, especially to his kids and grandkids. By then, we kids had heard all those stories so often we could repeat them from memory, but it was still fun to hear.

"Then, one summer afternoon," Peggy remembers, "Dad told us a story he had never told before. It was one of those hot days in August and the whole family was over at Dad's house. I remember the kids were in the living room with Grandpa, who had a cigar in his mouth as usual, and he started telling those old stories of his time on the railroad. My brother happened to walk through the room at that point and he kiddingly told my father that we had all heard those stories so often they were getting worn out. I don't think my father liked him saying that, so he took his cigar out of his mouth and pointed it at my brother and said, 'Then sit down on the couch and I'll tell you something I never told you kids.' "

Peggy relates that she and her brother, both somewhat abashed by their father's command, obediently sat down and started to listen. As Peggy now remembers, her father told them that one early morning in the spring of 1950 he was riding in the engine of a diesel locomotive on its way from Gary to Hammond. This was not an unusual run for his crew, who frequently were called on to shuttle freight cars between the two depots. On this morning, however, as they approached the outskirts of Hammond, they were notified by radio of a passenger train coming in behind them that needed immediate passage. They were ordered to switch their train over to the side-track and then to wait for the passage of the commuter train before returning to the main line and on into Hammond. Peggy remembers he father saying that this was a bit unusual and that the crew was not happy about the delay, yet they obeyed the directive and pulled their train a short distance up the tracks before stopping their progress.

"As my dad told the story, when they stopped the train that night and began to wait, he was up front in the cab with the engineer. As they talked about the day's events, just waiting for the go-ahead to proceed, suddenly they heard a scream from the ditch on the other side of the tracks. Dad said he looked at the engineer and gasped, 'What the hell was THAT?' and then both of them grabbed flashlights and scrambled down from the locomotive, thinking that someone was in trouble."

According to Peggy, her father related that as the men climbed out into the chill night air, shining their flashlights into the darkness, all seemed quiet and peaceful once again. Still unsure of what they had heard, the pair walked back down the line of cars, peering into the darkness of the Midwestern night. Hearing only the normal night sounds of crickets and the rustle of a gentle wind, they had turned to return to their cab when suddenly, according to Peggy's father John, "all hell broke loose."

"My dad said that as they turned to go back to the engine, suddenly a chorus of moans and screams filled the night around them. They all started up at once and he said the sound just overwhelmed them. It was not one but a whole chorus of people wailing and screaming. He said he distinctly heard a woman's voice right close to him screaming for help, and from the distance he could hear other voices just moaning without words. He said that it was like someone had opened the door to hell and let the sounds come out. He also said that in the background he could hear a muffled roar that he could not identify at first, but later he realized it sounded like the crackle of a huge bonfire burning. Yet all the time they could see nothing—just darkness beyond their flashlight beams."

John completed the tale for his wide-eyed family by saying that the sound lasted perhaps a minute as the two men stood dumbfounded on the tracks. Then, as mysteriously as they had begun, the sounds faded away. In the matter of a moment, the torrent of sound evaporated into the night mist.

"My dad said that they just stood there shining their flashlights into the weeds on the other side of the tracks, seeing nothing, and then without a word, they both just broke and ran back to the locomotive. He said that when they got back into the cab, the engineer was gray in the face and shaking. Dad reached for the radio but the engineer stopped him. 'I don't know what we just heard out there but we are not going to tell anybody about it', he insisted. Then he added, 'I have heard stories about this stretch of track and about what happens to people who talk about them. We are going to get the hell out of here and keep our mouths shut.' And that," Peggy concludes, "is just what my dad did for all of those years."

Other tales, too, have circulated around the tragedy site for many years. Vague tales are told of neighbors waking up in the early hours of the morning on the anniversary of the date of the accident to hear frantic pounding on their doors, as though someone were desperately seeking entrance. Inevitably, when the wary homeowner opened the door, no one was there.

At least one police report was reputedly filed in the 1960s when a local man, walking along the tracks one evening, was startled to see the figure of another person waving wildly to him by the side of the tracks. According to the story told, what made this sighting doubly macabre was that the figure before him seemed to be on fire.

It should be noted that not all who have worked the railroad, nor all those who live in the crash site area, believe the strange tales. Several current residents of the area report that despite many years of residence they have never heard such stories. Similarly, many long-time railroad workers are unaware of any workman ever reporting a strange occurrence on that section of the rails. However, those who have heard the stories remember them well—as dark, mysterious and chilling tales.

As the old adage states, it is darkest before the dawn. And in that darkness who knows what lies by the side of the railway junction just outside what was once the station at Ivanhoe? Perhaps it is nothing more than the sad memories of a tragic event. However, in the minds and recollections of some, there is the suggestion that there might be something more—dreadful remnants of a terrible night when death itself rode the rails.

NOTES

1. **"The Historic (Haunted) Kaske Mansion"**
   Mark Marimen, Personal Research and Interviews
   Munster Historical Society Archives.

2. **"The Spirits Of Wyandotte Cave"**
   Mark Marimen, Personal Research and Interviews
   "Wyandotte Cave Down Through The Centuries" by
      Angelo I. George, 1991, George Publishing Co.

3. **"The Prophet's Ghost, and Other Spirits of Tippecanoe"**
   Mark Marimen, Personal Research and Interviews
   "The Battle of Tippecanoe" by Reed Beard, 1911, Chicago Ill.
   "The Tipton Papers, Volume 1, 1809-1827" compiled by
      Glen A. Blackburn, 1942 Indiana Historical Bureau,
      Indianapolis.

4. **"The Restless Spirits of Hannah House"**
   Mark Marimen, Personal Research and Interviews
   "Haunted Heartland" by Beth Scott and Michael Norman,
      1985, Stanton and Lee Publishers.

5. **"Where Not All The Dead Rest In Peace"**
   Mark Marimen, Personal Research and Interviews.

6. **"When Darkness Comes to Central State"**
   Mark Marimen, Personal Research and Interviews
   State of Indiana Website, available at
      http://www.state.in.us/icpr/webfile/csh_aiin/chsintro.html

7. **"The Gentle Spirit of Kahler School"**
   Mark Marimen, Personal Research and Interviews
   "Kahler Ghost Tales," *Hammond Times,* October 22, 1993.

8. **"A Few Historic Ghosts of the Indiana Lake Region"**
Mark Marimen, Personal Research and Interviews
"Restoring the Glory," *Indianapolis Star,* September 22, 1997,
    Section E, page 1.

9. **"A Hoosier Banshee"**
Mark Marimen, Personal Research and Interviews.

10. **"When Death Came To The Big Top"**
Mark Marimen, Personal Research and Interviews
"No Performances Today" by Walter A. Reeder Jr., 1972,
    Hammond Historical Society. All quotations and photographs
    used by permission of the Walter Reeder estate.
"Chicago Haunts" by Ursual Bielski, 1998, Lake Claremont Press
"Chicago's Street Guide To the Supernatural" by Richard T. Crowe,
    2000, Carolando Press.

AFTERWORD

The midnight hour has passed once more. The fire has burned to embers, its soft glow darkening the shadows just outside our small circle of light. It is time, it seems, for us to part company once again.

Let me thank you once again for sharing this fire with me. Thanks also for sharing some of these stories. It is my hope that in them you have found some of the mystery, the wonder, and the magic that they have brought to me as I have collected them.

Now, it is time to return to the sanity of our beds. In a few hours the sun will rise again and we will go back to the "real" world. Yet, as you do, I hope that some vestige of this campfire will remain with you, as a reminder of those things that may well lie in the darkness just outside our circle of light.

As one of my favorite philosophers, Karl Koclhak, once remarked, "Sleep well, and before you do, try to tell yourself, '*It couldn't happen here…*' "

—MM, July 2001

Mark Marimen is interested in collecting more ghostly tales of Indiana. If you have a story you would like to share, you may contact him via Email at indianaghosts@hotmail.com. Mark Marimen is also available to speak to schools and assemblies as well as for interviews and book signings. Please contact him at the above address or at PO Box 44, Dyer Indiana, 46311-0044.